Jeannette Bu

Save **pounds** and the **planet**

Claire
for the best !

A Green Savings Guide that's Quicker, Cheaper, Easier

Saving the planet and your purse from your own home

I dedicate this book to my husband David, my daughter Daniella and to my mum, Marlen.

Foreword

When the author of this book, Jeannette Buckle, asked me to write a foreword I thought goodness how on earth do I do justice to her hard work?

However, on opening the book at any page, it is obvious that Jeannette has spent a lot of her time not only fully researching, cross referencing, but also ensuring that each and every fact or tip that is read indeed does work. Jeannette has, whilst putting together this exceptionally informative green guide, not only helped to save the planet, but the pounds in your pocket too. It is indeed a labour of love.

It is so easy to spend hours and hours merely dipping into the cornucopia of fascinating facts and tips that make up this unique book – but it is not time wasted! You are not only learning as you read how to be green, you are shown by the easy to understand icons on each and every tip or fact just what it offers.

Each chapter offers its own guiding principles and often there is not a lot of compromise, for you the reader, to achieve them yourself.

Relish spending your time going through the many interesting and informative facts, hints and tips. You will be pleasantly surprised how simple the changes are that you will have to make to create such a big difference not only to you, but your life, the pound in your pocket and importantly to our wonderful planet. A planet, that we will be pleased to hand on to our children and our children's children.

Enjoy!

Lesley Clarke OBE

Six things this book will help you do:

1   Save money

2   Reduce your impact on the planet

3   Know that your efforts, however small, are worthwhile

4   Be more aware of your lifestyle choices

5   Be a happier, greener and a more comfortable you

6   Help to create a calm, unpolluted environment

Contents

Content by Zones

Introduction

How this book works

This book is not about being perfect, it's about doing what you can when you can and showing that you can make a difference and save money.

This easy-to-use guide book will help you make small changes leading you to become more eco-friendly and more efficient, saving time, money and the planet. This book won't go into all the reasons why one way is better than another, and the feel-good factor will be there for you to discover for yourselves. This book is about getting down to the basics of what to do in as few words as possible. Some things you might already do; others you may not have thought of. One thing is for sure – the more you change, the more money you save. You might well think that these small changes will not amount to much, but as your grandmother probably said "take care of the pennies and the pounds will take care of themselves". The same is true for the planet. However small your changes are, they all add up. So you might well be a very small fish in an enormous sea, but you too can have a positive effect on our planet and your purse. As the adage says, think globally, act locally!

By following my tips you will save time, money and the planet, but by your actions you will also indirectly have a greater positive effect via the businesses, industries and utilities you influence by your lifestyle choices.

These knock-on effects of your reduced impact are not accounted for in this book, which concentrates only on your direct savings and actions. So remember there are more benefits both up and down the supply chain that you will not necessarily see, but the planet will notice. This is referred to as a product's **'Shadow'**– the hidden resources used such as energy, materials and water in production, packaging, distribution and disposal.

To add further substance to this book, I have done some research to check and back up my tips by what I feel are the most balanced and authoritative sources I could find in each case. These include some facts and figures about what you can save in financial terms. I find this very useful to focus the mind, and hopefully you will too. These sources are all referenced and detailed in the back of the book should you wish to do any further reading around a particular subject.

Still human

Let us not forget we are all human and that means we are not perfect –whatever 'perfect' is. Doing the 'right' thing in our daily habits is about making the best use of what we have and leading a normal life. Sometimes we will forget and sometimes we get stressed out and end up forgetting to recycle something or wasting food when we could have frozen it. Do not let that stop you; it happens to all of us from time to time. The important thing is that you continue to care for your planet and help your purse along the way.

This is only a guidebook, which I have written for 'normal' people leading 'normal' lives. That means that maybe you have children, eat meat, have a car, go on holiday by plane and have a hobby. Everything we do has an impact on the environment and the process starts every day with that first cup of tea. This book is not about how to make sacrifices – it is about how to maximise the benefits of what we have.

Take from the guide what you find useful and you think you can do once, some of the time or most of the time. It is all about everyone doing a little in the course of our daily lives, rather than just a few doing an extreme amount. Of course if you are one of those few, please do continue. To remind everyone this is a win-win situation I have drawn your attention to what you can save by placing savings symbols next to each tip.

Why I am writing this book

These are my suggestions that I accumulated over the years – suggestions of things you can do for your environment. My inspiration comes from childhood, where I was brought up to cook from fresh, not to waste food or throw stuff away and to repair things. It had nothing to do with saving money; it was just the 'right' thing to do. Later on I became a single working mum and I was glad to have an instinctive way of doing things that saved money without compromising my lifestyle.

Working in the environmental sector for over 24 years has given me added insight into waste and what happens to it. It became clear to me that we can all do a lot to reduce waste without compromising our quality of life, and that waste reduction was a comparatively untapped resource that lay outside mainstream thinking. Doing the right thing for the environment is common sense. It's not someone else's responsibility, it's everyone's. All you have to do at an individual level is ensure you are responsible for the facilities you use and the stuff you buy. Being sensible how you use water and energy and dispose of your waste is down to you and not just the preserve of your local council, the environmentalist or keen-and-green devotees. It should be normal and universally accepted; it should be the rule, not the exception.

Society is becoming more aware of conserving our countryside and the planet. It does not matter what background you come from or what job you do (if indeed you do any); this book highlights the sensible little everyday things that we can all do to make the most of our resources. Hopefully you do some of these things already, and if so, just keep doing them. But it would be wonderful if you would keep this book as a guide to try out some of the tips I have suggested, so you have even more ways to save your purse and planet.

Why Care?
Climate change
Climate change is clearly a fundamental international concern. As our planet's ambient temperature changes so does our climate, and this has potentially serious consequences—in terms of food production and natural disasters, for example. With over 63 million people in the UK (*World Bank, 2012*) and over 7 billion currently on the planet (*Worldometer, 2013*), it is clear if you stop and think about it that small changes to our weather patterns could cause floods

and droughts, rising sea levels and more in all regions across the world. With such a massive population, this can only put more pressure on our way of life, where we expect to have clean water on tap, energy for heat and light and all manner of foods to hand in the local shop.

Natural disasters and changes to the planet's climate went on long before man walked the Earth. There were times in the distant past when the Earth was warmer than it is now, for example. Over time the Earth might have looked and felt different to the world we know, due to global warming or even cooling, but ultimately our planet will survive.

On the face of it, global warming doesn't sound that bad. But human societies have developed and thrived during the relatively stable climate that has existed since the last ice age. (*Environmental Protection Agency, 2013*). As a consequence of the added effect of manmade greenhouse gases, global warming appears to be speeding up, and measurable changes are occurring in just decades. Global average temperature has increased by more than 1.4°F over the last century (*Environmental Protection Agency, 2013*). The issue is that humanity is believed to be collectively adding to this constant change in significant quantities, and therefore we can and should do something about it in order to preserve our way of life.

Also, with a huge and burgeoning population needing a constant supply of food and clean water, and where the majority of people live or aspire to live in an industrialised society, our processes and lifestyles will continue to put an increasing strain on the planet's resources. Added to this, there is currently a trend for long-term unsustainable consumption in the industrialised nations. As yet, the ability to enjoy the quality of life most of us would aspire to without compromising our environment still eludes mankind today. Hopefully in the future, we will overcome this issue.

I have hope...

What does this have to do with you?

There are many contributing factors to global warming, both natural and man-made. The focus in some countries is to at least reduce our man-made negative impacts to slow this process down. One such focus is reducing greenhouse gas emissions, which are a contributor to global warming.

Whatever we buy has been produced, and from cradle to grave there is a catalogue of environmental impacts that follows the lifecycle of everything we buy or use – from energy and water consumption to the use of natural resources and the way we treat discarded items and materials along the way. Ultimately, the final impact is what you as a consumer decide to purchase and how you use this item and finally dispose of it.

This is where you can really make a difference. Consider what you buy and how you use and dispose of it, and make informed choices. This does not just mean in your weekly shop but also in your home environment, your water and energy consumption and in your commitment to reduce and recycle your waste. It all helps to reduce your impact on the planet at no cost to you; in fact you will save money along the way.

66 *It is futile to do with more things that which can be done with fewer* 99

William of Occam c.1287-1347

Want to do more

For those really committed to doing more, this book is a starting point. A further suggestion would be investing in loft and cavity wall insulation. I have included some details on this to assist you as these are the steps that will give you the quickest return on your investment and therefore should be the first thing to do in terms of reduced heat loss and a consequent reduction in your energy consumption and bills.

You might even find it appropriate to generate your own electricity or hot water. If you do a lot of mileage it might be beneficial to buy a car with 'greener' credentials. These are all worthwhile and environmentally sound opportunities, but they usually require a capital investment and more often than not a number of years must pass before there is a financial saving. These are all great if you have the means, and if you are interested please do enquire about what else you can do. This book does not explore these technologies or approaches, but I would say it is worth checking if there are any subsidies for your home in your area – some might even be free, depending on your circumstances. Your local council can advise you on this or point you in the right direction.

If you want to find out more, you can find suggestions, further reading and links at the back of this book.

Navigating your way around the book

To help you find your way around the book, it is divided up into rooms and zones – so if you want to save on toiletries, look in Bathroom, if you want to find out more about food look in Kitchen or Shopping. Alternatively you can get straight to a key zone and look up Energy or Water, where you will find everything relating to savings in that category. In general, things that offer bigger savings and are easier to do are listed first in each subsection, so you will know where to start focusing your efforts. As we all make a huge impact on our finances and the planet when we are out of the house buying stuff, the best place to start changing our habits is while shopping. So I have dedicated a separate section for this, and begin with shopping, as it represents the best place to start reducing your impact.

Guide

Next to each tip are saving symbols so you know what you are saving with each habit change:

 Time = This means that you will save time on housework and general chores. I have not counted time as a cost saving but I have listed it, as I am sure you agree that any time saved is always a good thing—especially when it comes to chores!

 Money = No matter where you live—if it is English pounds you save, Euros, Dollars or Yen, cutting down on wastage saves you money no matter where you are in the world and helps reduce negative impacts on the environment.

 Energy = All Energy savings assume a typical 3 bedroom semi-detached house. Of course if you are not using your car you are saving energy in the form of reduced petrol costs. Amounts of money saved are taken from various sources available online in early 2013 to mid-2014, and use older data, so they are unlikely to reflect the current spike in energy bills, so you can safely assume they will save you at least the amount stated, if not a great deal more.

 Reduced rubbish = This means that you will save by not throwing away food or stuff unnecessarily, or you have purchased items with less packaging and therefore less impact on the environment and of course less carrying for you. Recycling actually saves time but initially if you are new to it you have to get into the habit before you really notice that it is easier as well as better. Also, by separating out all those 'Dry Recyclables' (paper, card, cans, glass bottles and jars, and plastic bottles, (including plastic food trays and tubs in some areas)) from other material, from which you can make compost, your rubbish bin will be less than one plastic sack a week and will **not** be smelly and unpleasant, a must to avoid in summer!

 Water = This book assumes you have to pay for the amount of water you use, so saving water saves money. If that doesn't apply to you yet, remember safe tap water, which is of drinkable quality, is not to be taken for granted. Even in England water shortages occur and hose pipe bans are put in place. There is no harm in getting into good habits and it will help the environment. All water savings are assuming a typical 3 bedroom semi-detached house.

Horrendous Household facts

I thought a bit of shock tactics with these horrendous household facts might help focus the mind. Visualising them will make your hair stand on end!

Shopping

'Of the total energy used in the food chain, 50% is used in food production and processing, 10% in transporting to the shop and retailing, 10% to make the packaging and the remaining 30% is used by us driving to the shops and storing and cooking food.' (*Incpen, 2006, p.6*).

Around '**600 million tonnes** of products and materials enter the UK economy each year... **only 115 million tonnes** of this gets recycled.' 'Nearly **25% of waste electrical and electronic equipment** (WEEE) that's taken to household waste recycling centres could be re-used, **worth around £200m gross a year**.' (WRAP, 2015)

Kitchen

'The average UK household is throwing away the equivalent of **six meals every week.** Wasted food and drink costs the average UK family **almost £60 a month**'. (*WRAP, 2013*)

The Guardian reported that the UK Soil Association, which sets standards for organic produce, has estimated that 20-40% of some UK fruit and vegetables are rejected because they are misshapen even before they reach the shops. (*theguardian.com, 2013*)

'The food sector accounts for 30 percent of all global energy consumption and 22 percent of total greenhouse gas emissions, according to the United Nations' Food and Agriculture Organization (FAO).' (*National Geographic, 2013*)

'Beef production, relying on large amounts of feed grain, is energy-intensive, with 40-to-1 fuel-to-food value in calories. On average, every calorie of food we consume uses up five calories of fossil fuel energy for pumping water, fertilising, harvesting, processing, transportation, and distribution.' (*National Geographic, 2013*)

'About two-thirds of the total aquifer water for irrigation is extracted through energy-intensive pumping from deep wells. That share is projected to rise to 87 percent by 2050, as shallower water reserves become depleted. Current extraction rates exceed the rate of recharge.' (*National Geographic, 2013*)

"In wealthy countries, about 210-250 pounds (95 to 115 kg) of food per capita is wasted annually, as fresh produce rots in the fridge, food is tossed after expiration dates, or left on the plate unconsumed. As a result, about 38 percent of global energy spent on food is wasted," says the United Nations FAO.' (*National Geographic, 2013*)

Bathroom

'Did you know that only 4% of the perfectly drinkable water you use every day is used for drinking? Or, that nearly a third of the water used in your home, is literally flushed down the toilet? What a waste!' (*Waterwise, 2013*)

'More than half (63%) our daily water consumption at home originates from the bathroom and the toilet' (*Waterwise, 2013*)

'If the entire adult population of England and Wales remembered to turn off the tap when they were brushing their teeth, we could save 180 mega litres a day - enough to supply nearly 500,000 homes and fill 180 Olympic swimming pools! (One Olympic sized pool is 1 million litres / 1Ml)' (*Waterwise, 2013*)

Laundry/utility room/housemaintenance

'Washing machines vary tremendously in how much water they use per wash: when adjusted for capacity, some use as much as 20 litres per kilogram while others as little as 6 litres per kilogram! Therefore, when buying a new washing machine it is important to make sure that the model is water efficient.' (*Waterwise, 2013, p.7*)

Bedrooms

'It has been estimated that every home in the UK could reduce the amount of energy it uses by 20%.' (*Act on Energy, 2013*)

Chill Out Room - Dining room/Lounge

'Over £6M electrical items are thrown away each year in the UK and it's estimated that over half are still working or could easily be repaired.' (*John Lewis department stores, WEEE leaflet, 2013*)

Home office

'On average a UK home spends between £45 and £80 a year powering electronic goods left in standby.' (*Energy Saving Trust, 2013*)

Garden

'Outdoor water use accounts for around 7% of the total water use, but in the summer this can rise to over 50% of peak demand.' (*Waterwise, 2013, p.1*)

A global view of giving

'The World Giving Index score is based on an average of three measures of giving behaviour - the percentage of people who in a typical month **donate money to charity, volunteer their time**, and **help a stranger**.

The 2014 report shows 'that giving is more than just about wealth, with only five G20 countries represented in the World Giving Index Top 20 – indeed, eleven G20 countries are even ranked outside of the WGI Top 50.' (Charities Aid Foundation, 2015)

Energy

'UK households are responsible for over 30% of the total carbon dioxide which is emitted into the atmosphere.' (*Act on Energy, 2014*).

In the UK three quarters of us overfill the kettle for our daily cuppa – costing Britain (all of us) a vast £68M a year! (*Energy Saving Trust, 2014*)

Water

'70% of the Earth is covered with water but only about 1% of the world's water is readily available for human use. Nearly 97% is salty or otherwise undrinkable. Another 2% is locked in the ice caps and glaciers. That leaves just 1% for all humanity's needs.

Each Briton uses about 150 litres of tap water a day, but if you include the amount of water embedded within products, our water consumption increases to about 3400 litres a day' (*Waterwise, 2013*)

Summary

10 guiding principles to always bear in mind for a happier, greener and more comfortable you, and which will ultimately help to create a calm unpolluted environment:

1. Only buy what you really need

2. Finish the last scrap

3. Turn it down and/or off

4. Save it and don't waste it

5. Fresh air is best

6. Don't spin it, hang it!

7. Cut down on chemicals

8. Less is more, think quality not quantity

9. Avoid buying items you can only use once

10. Repair, lease or buy second hand before buying new

Shopping

Principles

✓ Think of reasons not to buy things instead of justifying them

✓ Only buy what you really need

✓ Avoid buying items you can only use once

✓ Buy refillable and recyclable products

What you don't need to buy at all:

Of course there are exceptions relating to travel, personal circumstances and so on. The point is that if it's something you particularly enjoy then you don't have to sacrifice it to do your bit for the planet. This book allows you to think about your choices when you buy or when you use things— do you really need these things at all, or perhaps only some of the time? So start cutting down on these **'no fulfilment – no need'** items if you can:

No need to buy items:

Ready-made breadcrumbs, mineral and bottled water, compost/topsoil;

Freezer bags, bin liners, nappy sacks, plastic bags, non-rechargeable batteries, non-energy saving light bulbs;

Paper napkins, paper towels, paper cups and plates, paper handkerchiefs,

Patio heater, garden sprinkler, leaf blower;

Air fresheners, fabric softeners, an array of various cleaners, mouthwash, shower gel, wet-wipes, moist-lets, baby-wipes, cotton wool

What you can buy less of/use very little of:

Cleaning products, cling film, baking foil, matches, paper, disposable nappies, cotton buds, disposable paper toiletries, water, fizzy drinks, junk snacks/food, ready-meals/ part prepared foods, processed foods, ...

...If you are having your doubts about what you can do without or how you can do things a different way, I would say read this book and experiment before you decide. For me it all boils down to quality of life. Everyone has a certain amount of money to spend; the question is where your priorities are. I would rather spend as little as possible on those no fulfilment items and more on enjoyment. So the choice is yours—a well-stocked cupboard full of cling film and air fresheners or more days or nights out; tickets to the local show, dinner in a restaurant, socialising with friends, holidays – whatever you decide.

The weekly shop

Principles

✓ Use up the old before buying new

✓ Avoid the urge to buy stuff you don't really need

Horrendous Household fact:

'Of the total energy used in the food chain, 50% is used in food production and processing, 10% in transporting to the shop and retailing, 10% to make the packaging and the remaining 30% is used by us driving to the shops and storing and cooking food.' (Incpen, 2006, p.6).

The things highlighted above show that there is a huge amount you can do to reduce your energy consumption. The same is true of water consumption and waste, all of which will save you money too. Below I have given you some food for thought which will hopefully help you with those lifestyle changes and to stock your cupboards more wisely, with less waste and more quality.

The curse of the plastic bag is a particular pet hate. Why they end up discarded and thrown about our streets and left in our beautiful countryside I cannot begin to understand. It could simply be that if you don't have to pay for something, people think it has no value and therefore it is treated as disposable. I have written a list of useful things you can do with them to delay their journey to the dustbin.

Make a list

Make a list before you go and stick to it.

Bring your own shopping bags

Either take your old plastic bags and reuse them, or bring some cloth or other reusable bags or baskets to avoid paying for them at the shop. Even if bags are free it is still better to take your own whenever you can.

Don't go out and buy a tote cotton bag or similar or a paper bag, just use bags that you already have. Remember every bag (paper ones included) also has an environmental impact in its production. It is better to reuse something than replace it.

Plastic bags get a bad press because they are a nuisance in terms of litter and damage to wildlife, so for that reason I avoid taking them home as much as possible and make sure they are disposed of properly.

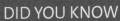

DID YOU KNOW

'On average each adult uses a frightening 300 plastic bags each year, each bag remaining in the environment for decades or even centuries. Thousands upon thousands of birds, whales, dolphins, seals, turtles etc. suffer and die as a result of discarded plastic bags each year.

(Plastic Bag Free Chesham, 2007)

Drinking Water

No need to buy bottled water. The best and most affordable water to drink is tap water in the UK. The least affordable option is bottled water. A water filter is better than buying bottled water if you feel you need one.

| Drinking Water *(continued)* | UK tap water is perfectly safe for drinking. It is also stringently tested and regulated, (*Water UK, 2013*) so for me it is the safer option, and saves money and unnecessary carrying too. . | |

| Water sports | We all need to keep properly hydrated and this is most important when playing sports. Instead of a buying a new water bottle, go for a sturdier reusable screw-top one and fill it with tap water. Or use your old plastic plain water bottle. (*Don't leave it in the sun or rolling around in the back seat of the car*). | |

| What's for dinner | Look in the fridge and larder first to see what needs to go and then buy ingredients around it to make a meal. | |

| Trying to tempt | If you buy certain foods hoping the family is going to eat them this time (Brussels sprouts or that healthy melon, perhaps) you could just be feeding your bin. So try an alternative healthy food instead that will not get wasted, or buy a frozen option you can eat a little at a time. | |

| Avoid the urge | Instead of justifying buying something, do the opposite; think of reasons why you don't really need it. | |

Fruit and Veg

Buy Loose. Less packaged/prepared foods usually cost less.

The sooner you eat a fruit or vegetable after it's picked, the better it is in terms of nutrient content so the better value for money too. (*WebMD, 2013*)

Avoid peeled, chopped and washed varieties. It saves you a few minutes, but you pay for it and it costs you in depleted nutrients too. Cutting fruits and vegetables reduces some of the nutrients— such as vitamin C—when the flesh is exposed to the oxygen in the air. (*nutrition.about.com, 2013*)

Try to avoid taking extra bags. Price tags after weighing can go on your melon, bananas etc.

Frozen, canned or fresh

Buy only enough fresh food that you know you can eat.

Frozen vegetables are often just as healthy as fresh vegetables, especially if you do not eat the ones you buy straight away, and are therefore good value for money. Frozen vegetables are still nutritious, because they often come right out of the field and are blanched and frozen immediately. The same can be said for canned. (*WebMD, 2013*)

Preserves

These can sit in the cupboards and fridges too long, so open just one jam jar at a time to avoid them going off. To finish the jar more quickly, use it to cook with if it's been open for a while.

Buy one get one free - beware!

Be careful when buying these. If it is not something you regularly buy, it is likely not to be worth your while. Stockpiling shampoo is extreme. There's no need to go overboard, but having one spare as there is an offer on is sensible.

BOGOF

Buy one get one free on fresh food could mean Buy one throw two away! Be careful when buying fresh food items. If you are not sure you will eat it that day or the next at the latest, it
will probably go in the bin. Instead of saving, you're spending money to feed the bin! Decide to use within 3 days or cook and freeze straight away and stick to it. Better to defrost something you could have had fresh than throwing food away.

Buy in season

When buying food such as fruit, vegetables, meat and fish buy what's in season where you live. This way you are more likely to get fresher food at a better price, locally grown. This saves a fortune in food miles (the transportation from field to fork) and provides you with a fresher apple. Most of us don't know when local food is in season—but do not fear, I have it here! see summary below from Love British Food where I have listed a few of the most useful foodstuffs to help you plan your meals and get some variety:

Spring –   Rhubarb, gooseberries, asparagus, broccoli, spring greens, Spinach.
            Haddock, lamb.

Summer –   Plums, currants, berries.
            Beetroot, broad beans, courgettes, tomatoes, salads, beans.
            Crab, pilchards, beef, pork.

Autumn –   Apples, blackberries.
            Mushrooms, squashes, lettuce, marrow.
            Skate, brill, ham, pork.

Winter –   Pears, apples.
            Brussels sprouts, cabbage, leeks, parsnips.
            Red mullet, mussels, all birds & turkey, gammon.
            (*Love British Food, 2013*)

Buy in season
(continued)

You can always buy food out of season nowadays, but it is more expensive as a rule due to increased production costs, even if local. That means your strawberries will cost more in December than in June.

Buy local

Buy from local markets that sell locally grown produce. Farmers' markets are great, because usually you get produce the day after it was harvested and it is therefore healthier, fresher and better value. *(WebMD, 2013)* To find your local farmers' market search online *(Local Farmers Markets (2007)*.

Other everyday market items can be cheaper than the supermarket. I prefer them to organic food flown in from far away. Some markets stalls can be expensive, so be choosy, but bargains are to be had—especially in the afternoon when they want to shift their stock.

If you buy in the supermarket you can also choose more local food to support growers in your region. This moves the debate to supporting the local economy and self-reliance. It also touches on ensuring we maintain the skills and ability to grow our own food, produce our own energy, supply clean water and have the manufacturing and engineering expertise to sustain your way of life. It is not about being against foreign goods and services, which we are all reliant on, but about not losing the capabilities in your country.

Only buy what you know you will use

Ideally if fresh, buy what you will use up within 3 days. Cook what is left and freeze it for another day. Remember the longer you wait to eat those vegetables the fewer nutrients they contain. *(WebMD, 2013)*

Buy meat and fish from your local butcher or fishmonger or from the counter at the supermarket	Less packaging and normally like for like cheaper. Also you can buy only what you need. The same goes for fish. Buy just enough meat and/or freeze the rest in portion sizes.	

Healthy means wealthy	In theory we should eat about 100 grams of protein each at meal times, but the reality is that as a general rule we eat much more. As well as the negative health effects of eating too much of something, unnecessary food will add a huge amount to your food bill, especially when buying more meat than needed. Also you will be less healthy and therefore need potentially more medicines and trips to the doctor or dentist, all of which costs money. Below are the health guidelines from the *UK National Health Service* (NHS) to help you make savings where you are spending too much money, and to remind you what you need more of. Hopefully you can save a few pounds or perhaps Euro's along the way by making all your calories count. A meal should contain about one third vegetables or fruit, one third starchy food like bread, cereals, potatoes, rice or pasta, and the remaining third a mixture of milk and dairy products or other protein sources such as meat, fish, eggs and beans. You can add a small amount of sugary or high-fat foods. *(NHS, 2013)*	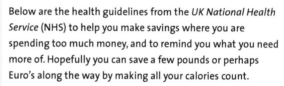

Vegetarian green tips	Meat and fish are usually more expensive than other foods and a far greater drain on the planet's resources than crops such as fruit, vegetables and starchy foods like rice and pasta. Reviewing what you eat will really save you a serious amount on your weekly shop.	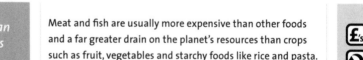

? DID YOU KNOW

'*Because methane has more than 20 times the global warming potential of carbon dioxide, the digestive methane emissions from ruminants like cattle help to make livestock production more greenhouse-gas intensive than either crop production or other stages of the food-supply chain.*' (National Geographic, 2013).

Beware of ready meals/ part prepared/ processed food

Buy raw ingredients instead and cook. Wash and chop veg/fruit/salad yourself, it's healthier and tastes better.

For convenience, ingredients such as frozen meat and vegetables that you cook are a better alternative.

Breadcrumbs

No need to buy readymade breadcrumbs. Just make sure you keep any leftover bread and let it go stale and dry. Then use a rolling pin or food processor to make instant bread crumbs ready to use.

Paper cups and plates

Avoid buying single use items, such as paper cups and plates; instead use durable and washable plastic ones.

Plastic bags

Even with best intensions we all have too many plastic bags, so there is really no need to buy rolls of them. There are alternatives listed throughout the book, so take them out of the trolley, you will not need them!

Free Plastic bags

Reduce the amount of plastic bags you use in the supermarket. In self-serve supermarkets, weigh the food and put the price sticker directly onto melons, bananas etc. There is no need to put them into a plastic bag. The same goes for all fruit and veg including carrots. Just stick the label on one of them and the cashier will get the idea. For mushrooms use the paper bags provided as you can recycle or compost them easily—and most importantly mushrooms keep better in a paper bag.

If you wish you can bring spare plastic bags from home for your loose fruit and veg, as well as bigger ones for all your shopping.

I do all of the above and have for years and to my surprise I have never yet run out of bags!

Nappies

Nappies for a short period of time in your life are a big debate as to what is best - cotton or disposable.

There are lots of arguments environmental and financial on either side and there is no clear-cut winner, as it depends on so many different personal circumstances. Search local options and compare prices, but clearly the sooner potty trained the less shopping, water and energy use and therefore money saved.

Nappy sacks

No need to buy nappy sacks. They are covered in plastic already so just seal up with the nappy tape and stick in the black bin. If you feel you need to use an additional bag an old supermarket plastic bag or any other plastic bag you have in the house if you think you need to put them in a sack will do.

Bin liners

No need to buy bin liners. Use the spare plastic bags you have around the house to line your pedal bin.

If your council requires you to have a black bag for household waste collection, try to minimise your black bag waste by recycling as much as you can to avoid the need for so many black plastic bags.

Buy in Bulk

Buy in bulk when you can – but beware of those "offers" I mentioned above! For non-perishable or long shelf life items buying in bulk will be cheaper per kilo, and contain less packaging, potentially less trips in the car and time saved.

For fresh food, freeze the surplus on day of purchase for later use.

But beware: If you buy more meat than you need just because the price is slightly cheaper per pound this is only a saving if you put that meat aside and freeze it, not if you eat more than you need or would do normally.

Remember you're paying for it all

Whatever you buy you are paying for everything you leave with i.e. the box, wrapping and extras, so take note of those apples, chocolates with extra wrapping.

For whatever you buy check the price per gram/ kilo, not the price of the packet! You might buy a bigger box of tea, but have you checked the cost per cup?

The same applies to toiletries and cosmetics.

Go in pairs

If you do your supermarket shop with a friend or relative, you can potentially save more and perhaps have a chat and a cup of coffee with some of your savings afterwards – much more fun.

You can make further savings by taking advance of the buy one get one free offers and buy in bulk meat/fish offers that don't taste so good once frozen or you do not have enough freezer space. Just figure out how you are going to settle up before you go.

Going in pairs and sharing the car journey saves fuel and parking charges. Much more fun.

Parking: park nearest the exit and not the front door of the shop. It saves petrol, and those few steps more are good for you and will probably be less stressful parking as you will always find a space quicker.

See the driving tips below.

Driving tips

You can save 10% on your weekly fuel bill by just taking a little bit more care, *advises the Automobile Association in their Eco-Driving advice*: When you get in the car, turn the engine on last not first. Don't leave the engine on when in standing traffic or waiting to pick someone up when safe to do so.

Drive smoothly when slowing down and speeding up. Change up a gear as soon as you can, but without the engine complaining about it (2000 – 2500rpm).

In slow moving traffic it is better to keep moving very slowly then stopping and starting.

There is no need to coast the car (take out of gear) as we did years ago with old cars – this is also dangerous.

Driving tips
(continued)

Remember, don't carry unnecessary stuff in your car; it increases the weight. Increasing drag with items such as roof racks all adds to fuel consumption so remove roofracks when not needed. Also keep all the electrics turned off, and just turn on when needed—air con, windscreen heaters, blowers and headlights, radio.

Ensure you service the car and check tyre pressures regularly to ensure efficient running. Check you are using the right engine oil.

The faster you go the more fuel you use. Cruising at 80mph instead of 70mph can use up to 25% more fuel. *(AA, 2013)*

Carton or plastic bottle

I often get asked which is best and it is not a clear-cut answer, so buy whichever gives you the most product, such as juice or milk, for your money. Not everywhere has carton recycling but transporting goods in cartons usually uses less space on the lorry and therefore less fuel in transportation. Pick items with plastic packaging made out of HDPE or PET, which are easily recyclable. Other products might not be recyclable in your area, even if they have the recycling logo on them!

Buy refillable and recyclable

Buy refillable and recyclable products when you can and remember to reuse them. Less packaging usually means less cost.

The same goes for the packaging. Buy items that are packaged in things you can easily recycle, a great way to slim your bin!

If you DARE

Leave any non-essential wrapping at the checkout, especially if you cannot recycle it. In the long run the shop will get the hint and do something about the unnecessary packaging. Less for you to carry home too.

General shopping

Principles

✓ Walk when you can

✓ Do your research

✓ Less is more

Horrendous Household fact:

*Around '**600 million tonnes** of products and materials enter the UK economy each year... **only 115 million tonnes** of this gets recycled.' 'Nearly **25% of waste electrical and electronic equipment (WEEE)** that's taken to household waste recycling centres could be re-used, **worth around £200m gross a year.**' (WRAP, 2015)*

There is a lot that you can do without feeling you have to compromise. Simple things like walking to the shops or parking away from the congested part of town and walking in, all help to reduce your impact on the planet and reduces your own stress at the same time. Now, in the Internet Age, you can browse online to choose what you buy and of course you can sell your unwanted items too. Online businesses provide anything from car insurance to bank accounts and cut out on unnecessary paperwork, postage and mileage for you and your supplier. This all adds to less clutter, which makes your home environment more pleasant. Quite simply the less stuff we receive the less we have to do in terms of admin, cleaning, sorting out, binning and recycling.

Less is more. Really the best place to start is to ask yourself if you really need to buy something at all. Could you borrow it, use something else you already have instead, check you haven't got another one in the cupboard somewhere, or perhaps you can repair it? Another alternative is to trade or swap it.

Transport

How about not using the car all the time to run those errands? Great for when you are just buying a few fresh items for dinner.

Swapping the car for the bike or walking is a wonderful way of relaxing and lifting your mood, and the exercise is great for you and your family's health. Hopefully this will save you sitting in traffic and it might well be quicker and less stressful, as well as saving you petrol and car maintenance.

If you go by car, avoid rush hours to save queues, petrol and time or a car share might work too.

Do all your short errands at the same time, so do the shopping on the way home from work or after the school run, if you have children. Or even better, join or organize a walking bus for the school run saving you time and money.

See driving tips in the previous section to save you 10% on your weekly fuel bill.

Bills

Switch to paperless bills and direct debits, as these are usually cheaper as they give you incentives to reduce administration costs. Read your meter readings for gas and electricity to ensure you are not paying more than you are using. Compare energy suppliers, as you might be able to get a better deal elsewhere – but remember to check the small print.

Worth buying then worth repairing

Once something is broken, repair it or get it repaired before considering replacing it.

Repair clothes where possible to extend their natural lives.

Replacing things

Think first – do I really need to replace, or could I use something else instead? If you need to buy, consider water and energy running costs before purchasing. Even better, think about buying reconditioned, second hand or hiring items.

Hire

Think about hiring before buying. Join the library and borrow books, games, DVDs, CDs and magazines. In your local area you might even have a local toy library, which is ideal if you have kids.

Instead of buying specialist DIY tools you will not use very much, hire something ideal for the job and return it, saving time and money.

Electrical appliances

If you are planning on buying a new fridge-freezer for example, choosing an Energy Saving Trust recommended model could save you around £89 on energy bills over the lifetime of the appliance. Look out for the logo on all electrical items, from cars to kettles. (*Energy Saving Trust, 2013*)

If buying new or second hand equipment, make sure it has the energy saving trust logo on it and check the rating. Choose ideally an A+++ rating for the most energy efficient. You can work out the whole cost to run the appliance as well as buying it, to make sure you get the best overall deal. Read the small print to find out what the running costs will be and compare before you buy.

Ensure you get your old electrical items recycled.

The easiest way is to get advice from the shop you are buying from –they may even provide a collection service or take your old appliance to your local council *Household Waste Recycling Site* if you are not selling, donating to charity or freecycling it.

For more information on Freecycling see separate item at the end of this section and see Freecycle link at the back of the book.

Batteries

Batteries contain heavy metals such as mercury, lead, cadmium, and nickel, which can contaminate the environment when batteries are improperly disposed of. One way to reduce the number of batteries in the waste stream is to purchase rechargeable batteries. (*EPA, 2015*)

Buying rechargeable batteries is the most cost effective.

'Recharging a pack of four AA batteries 100 times using our Best Buy charger will cost around £91 (including the cost of the charger).

For 400 AA disposable batteries you'd pay £100 to £499.'
(*Which?, 2015*)

Home improvements

If you want to modernize your bathroom or kitchen there is no need to rip everything out and start again. You can reuse the kitchen cabinet bases, just replace with a new worktop or doors. Often it is about changing the layout to suit your needs and just a new worktop will do the trick. Remember to offer what you rip out to someone else, either to buy or to pick up for free. You can do this online or on a local notice board, if you do not know anyone who might be interested consider *freecycle*.

Water consumption

When buying new appliances, remember to ensure they are the most water efficient ones. As well as saving the planet you will be saving on water and energy bills, as the less water you use the less you need to heat. A good example of this is when buying a new shower head. For more information on this, see the bathroom section.

New and stylish

If you do choose to buy something new, you can also buy something stylish and on trend as well as being kinder to the planet—anything from sustainable wood furniture to bamboo fluffy towels and scarves. For further information search ethical clothing online. See link at the back of the book for *Fashion-conscience.com*.

Handkerchiefs

A great opportunity to buy and use material handkerchiefs instead of disposable paper ones, and gentler on your nose. Add to your whites wash.

Toys

Toy libraries are also a great place to find toys suitable for your children. Ideal when growing up fast and growing out of various creative play toys. Look online under toy libraries to find one near you.

Swap for it

Kids have done this for years, but it's not just about clearing out your cupboard to find 7 school rulers and swapping them for pencils or rubbers. Now adults too can swap. There are various websites providing this service and you can even 'Swish' your clothes.

Swishing is where you arrange for your friends to come round for nibbles and drinks, but instead of kitchen products or makeup, everyone brings clothes they can't fit in to or items they don't want any more and if you like you swap clothes or items. This is also an opportunity to think about altering clothes while your friends are there to help you decide. *(Futerra Sustainability Communications Ltd, 2014)*

Don't bin it

Shops will soon be able take your old electrical items (even if they are not working) free of charge when buying a new one from them. This could apply to anything you buy in a shop and even now you can give mobiles, glasses, old medicines to appropriate shops where they will donate them to a good cause for reuse or recycling. Some might even give you money off other products or vouchers.

See a few sources in the bibliography at the back of the book.

Cosmetics

The key is to follow one simple rule—finish what you have before you buy new. This will help clear the clutter over time all by itself.

Cosmetics can range from cheap to eye-wateringly expensive, be it lipstick, moisturizers, eye creams and so on. The key is to buy the less harsh chemical varieties, which will be kinder to your skin and the planet. There are various ethical brands out there that combine the desire to provide more natural and organic products.

These more caring companies are usually more likely to avoid animal testing and reduce their carbon emissions from packaging choices to production techniques.

Clothes and shoes

Buy quality, not quantity. You will save in the long run. Don't forget swishing as mentioned above for a new look.

If you are clearing out old clothes, make sure you take them to a charity shop or a charity bank. If they are not good enough to sell, they will still make use of them either to those in need abroad or sold to industry for reprocessing. Once you have put them in the bin they cannot be recovered, so please avoid doing this.

Clothes and shoes
(continued)

Ethical brands are also now cropping up, so you can buy with the assurance that you are not creating any unnecessary damage to the environment or wildlife or the welfare of communities. Visit online sites that also stock the latest trends.

Hire clothing instead of buying when you know you wouldn't get much wear out of it. This is a great way to stay on trend with the latest fashions and have room in your wardrobe. Weddings, the races, balls and parties are the obvious opportunities to hire clothing, but you can also hire when pregnant.

Borrowing from a relative or friend can work too. For example my husband has a dinner suit which fits my brother, so he borrows it from time to time and gets it dry-cleaned. A win for both sides.

Second hand

Buy second hand. You can come across some great bargains – a new pasta maker, fruit bowls, clothes and toys. Ideal places are charity shops, fetes, car-boot sales, reconditioned furniture shops, online or even auctions.

Top soil/ compost

No need to buy; make your own. It's free and easy and good for your garden. See garden section for more details.

Freecycle

Freecycle is an online site where you can find items for free in your area for you to collect. People post details of items they want or items they are offering. You can find anything from a single bed to a printer. It is also a good way to donate stuff you don't need any more that needs collecting, such as furniture. *The Freecycle Network (2013).*

Kitchen
How to save with food...

Principles

✓ Do not waste food

✓ Healthier means wealthier

✓ Use up every scrap

✓ Cut down on chemicals

Horrendous Household fact:
'The average UK household is throwing away the equivalent of six meals every week. Wasted food and drink costs the average UK family almost £60 a month' (WRAP, 2013).

They say the kitchen is the most expensive room in the house. The statement usually refers to the kitchen units, appliances and worktops. But it is probably the most wasteful room in the house too. All too often we forget what is in the fridge, and it goes off. Add that up over a year and you could have an average bill of £720 per year for nothing! Quite frankly I would rather spend the money on a nice weekend break than set another place at the dinner table for the pedal bin!

From an environmental viewpoint, keep organic matter (anything that decomposes) out of landfill. The decomposition of waste in the absence of air (e.g. in a landfill) produces methane gas, which is over 21 times more potent as a greenhouse gas than CO_2, (United States Environmental Protection Agency, 2014) so it's well worth keeping organic matter out of the black bag bin from an environmental point of view, aside from the waste of money.

Below are some tips that will help you avoid waste from all perspectives, from wasting food, reducing packaging and wasting money.

There are also loads of tips on how to store food so as not to waste it and cut down on cooking time and cleaning, all of which saves money.

Before we start please ensure your fridge or freezer is not next to the cooker or central heating boiler, as this will make it hard work for the fridge or freezer to stay cool.

Food tastes better than pills!

If you eat a proper diet, why do you still need supplements? Below is an informed comment by the NHS. Take note, as you can save a lot of money if you cut down on unnecessary pills.

'Vitamins and minerals are essential nutrients your body needs in small amounts to work properly.

Most people should get all the nutrients they need by eating a varied and balanced diet. If you choose to take vitamin and mineral supplements, be aware that taking too many or taking them for too long can cause harmful effects.' (NHS, 2013)

Use by and best before dates

Dates on food packaging can be confusing. Sell and display by dates are for the shop staff.

You need to be mindful of use-by dates for fresh food, as this food could go off when past this date. This is especially important for meat, fish or dairy. Use your common sense, even when within the use-by date. Always check that the food looks and smells fine. Eggs can be eaten a few days after the use by date as long as they are cooked thoroughly. (WRAP, 2013)

Best before dates are exactly that, telling you the quality might not be so good in terms of taste or texture after that date. It does not mean it is harmful, so you don't necessarily need to throw it out after that date. Check the small print if in doubt. (WRAP, 2013)

Dates to hand or not, check it doesn't look or smell off and always cook thoroughly. If in doubt, I would advise not feeding it to the old, the young or the pregnant.

My lunch usually consists of what 'needs to go' and leftovers. I tend to make sure it is piping hot and this must have saved a small mountain of food being wasted over the years.

Organize	Ensure you eat the oldest food first by putting new supplies at the back of the fridge or cupboard. This goes from anything from carrots to pots of jam.	
Fruit bowl syndrome	Don't over-buy and don't put out too much at once. Only refill once emptied. If a piece of fruit has developed a bruise, eat it first, cutting out the offending bit. Once fruit has lost its appeal, cut out rotten parts and turn into smoothies, salads or cook and freeze. Use in crumbles, sauces, flambé fried bananas on ice cream; the possibilities are endless.	
Buy in season	See what is in season from fruit and veg and even meat and fish in the weekly shop section above.	
Hang out with grapes	When grapes have lost their appeal but are not mouldy, hang them to dry in a fresh, warm area. You will have sultanas for the picking in a few weeks. Just keep an eye on them and remove any that go mouldy. They can stay there until you are ready to use.	
Going Bananas	Do not put bananas in the fruit bowl with other fruit, as they tend to speed up the ripening of other fruit which can result in those fruits going off sooner than expected. (*Fyffes, 2013*) Bananas don't taste so good when stored in the fridge so buy in smaller quantities and leave out.	

Storing fruit and veg

If you keep fruit and veg in the fridge they will usually keep longer, but to get the most out of them here are some handy tips which are ideal when you are running out of space in your fridge from the *Edinburgh Community food website*

Keep all fruit and veg out of direct sunlight.

Don't store onions and potatoes together, keep them separate.

As a rule it is best not to display a variety of fruits together in a bowl as a lot of fruit—including apples, tomatoes and avocado—produce ethylene when they are ripe, speeding up the ripening of all other fruits near them and so reducing their longevity. (*Edinburgh Community Food, 2013*)

Best in the fridge

Green and leafy green vegetables are best kept in the fridge, as are most vegetables including root vegetables including leeks, courgette, broccoli, cauliflower, corn, artichoke, asparagus, grapes, apples, cantaloupe and honeydew melon.

All berry fruits are best in the fridge, stored in a single layer, as are apricots and figs.

When storing in the fridge keep your vegetables and fruit separate and keep them in their perforated plastic bags and mushrooms in their paper bags. (*Edinburgh Community Food, 2013*)

I prefer to put potatoes, peppers and aubergine in the fridge as I think they last longer.

Best out of the fridge

As a rule, hot coloured fruit and vegetables with a thick skin do better out of the fridge. These include watermelon, squash, pineapple, avocado, ginger and garlic along with citrus fruit, tomato, mango, cucumber, bananas.

Once ripe you can put some fruits in the fridge to last a bit longer: avocado, kiwi, nectarine, peach, pear and plum. (*Edinburgh Community Food, 2013*)

These guidelines assume you live in an English climate or similar. If you live in a hot humid climate in my experience everything goes in the fridge except watermelon.

Best out of the fridge
(continued)

Having said all this, I tend to put most things in the fridge if I have space except onions, citrus fruits and bananas as it is just more convenient for me. I tend to buy and use them up within 7 days for fresh fruit and veg as a rule even if they are in the fridge.

If buying loose store them in a cotton sack, like the thick cotton shopping bag ones you can get.

When space is short in the fridge these fruits and vegetables can be taken out first to make room for something else.

Transform cucumbers

If you have spare fresh cucumber and you don't want to waste it, pickle it. You can do this simply by slicing the cucumber and putting them in a glass jar. Cover cucumbers with vinegar from an existing jar of pickles and wait 24 hours. Consume within a couple of weeks. Once eaten use the vinegar for cleaning and not for another batch of pickles. Or make your own pickling vinegar by adding herbs such as dill and peppercorns and coriander seeds. It is quick and easy to do. For a professional touch and for it to keep for much longer follow a recipe.

Revive Carrots

If your carrots have gone a bit bendy, to bring them back to their crispy good selves put them in a glass of water in the fridge, and they will be as good as new before you know it. You can do the same with cucumbers too. *(WRAP, 2015)).*

Storing herbs

Herbs keep best in a glass of water. Trim the ends and stand on the worktop away from direct sunlight like you would a bunch of flowers. To make them last even longer, place the herbs in their glass in the fridge and cover with a loose plastic bag. Store asparagus in the same way in the fridge. If you don't have room, wrap asparagus in a damp tea towel in the fridge. Basil is best stored out of the fridge.

(Edinburgh Community Food, 2013)

| **Fruit and veg from the garden** | If you have an apple tree like I do or a lot of one type of fruit or vegetables the best advice is to peel, slice, blanch and freeze as much as you can to avoid any wastage. Of course you can also make pickles and jam too – and let's not forget endless excuses for homemade crumbles. Yum, yum. Apples store quite well in the fridge too, in the bottom drawers. | |

| **Citrus fruit** | If you have bought too many lemons or other citrus fruit, freeze in slices to use another day or in cooking. If they become too dried out, use them for cleaning. | |

Onions

If you don't need to use a whole onion just cut off what you need and put the remainder, with outer skin on, in the bottom drawer of the fridge to use over the next few days (store separate from any fruits).

If you have too many onions, or you don't need a whole one, or you just want to cut down on tears and time, or if you think you are not going to use the sack of onions you have bought, or to save time later and avoid them going off, just chop them up finely ready for use and freeze. You can then just shake out a few at a time that way you waste no part of the onion and save loads of time in preparation.

Really handy tip when you don't want to redo your makeup!

Potatoes

If you have cooked too much mashed potato, you can freeze some for another day, or store in the fridge and use within two days. Likewise you can peel, slice and blanch potatoes and then freeze ready for another day to use as sautéed or fried potatoes or in a potato salad – an ideal time saver for weekdays. It also helps keep your freezer stocked and dinner on hand if you forget to buy fresh and have run out.

Fizzy drinks	I don't see the need or any benefit in them. I have water instead, and perhaps a little wine now and then. If I want a sweet drink I would make my own by mixing water with homemade fruit juice or even easier squeeze half an orange or dash of lemon juice into a glass and top up with water.	

Sports drinks	Sports drinks are usually drunk when exercising hard. You can make your own at the fraction of the cost as follows: Put 20-40gms of sugar, a pinch of salt, and one litre of warm water (to dissolve the sugar) into a water bottle, replace lid and shake and you are ready to use. If you wish you can add a squirt or two from a lemon or orange. It's surprisingly sweet with or without, and you can replace sugar with fruit squash (*BUPA UK, 2013*).	

Tea bags	You can reuse these to make another mug of tea, which will halve your tea bag costs. Ideal if you do not like very strong tea, like me. Put used teabags into a kitchen home composting container afterwards, if you have one.	

Takeaways	This is an expensive way of feeding the family at home without any of the fun of going out. Instead it would be cheaper to treat the whole family to fillet steak and all the trimmings. Food for thought.	

Packaged meals

Ready meals or part-prepared food might be quicker, but they mean more cost. Also you have to consider that they might not be as nutritious as a home-cooked meal. Buy raw ingredients instead and pre-cook meals yourself for those times when you know you will be in a hurry. You can buy frozen ingredients such as vegetables and meat/fish, so you don't always have to go to the shops. Most meals only take half an hour or less to prepare from scratch.

Dinner for one

Just because it's only you for dinner, you can still eat well without the pre-prepared premium. Just cook all the vegetables in one pot along with the carbohydrates. It takes a few seconds to peel and chop for one. Or microwave a plate of leftovers; it takes just 3 minutes. You can make more than one portion of a dish at the weekend and freeze in portion sizes to use during the week if you like, too.

Leftovers

Freeze leftovers straight away, or eat them within two days so there's no waste. Freeze into portion sizes to ensure no waste.

A plate of food can be kept in the fridge (covered) for 2-3 days, (Food Standards Agency, 2015). Then simply reheat as you would a ready meal in the microwave accordingly depending on make and model, if unsure for 3 minutes per plate at full power to ensure piping hot is enough for an old model.

Rice is not as harmless as it looks. It needs careful handling. Treat it as if it were meat when cooking and storing, then you won't go far wrong.

Make sure re-heated food is properly cooked through. If reheating the next day do not leave at room temperature, store in the fridge and cover, and cook till piping hot the next day. (NHS, 2013)

Hungry before or after dinner

Instead of snacking after dinner, cook more dinner. Perhaps add a healthy starter or pudding. Or if snacking before, cook dinner earlier. It's cheaper than snacks. If you do go for something before or after, grab for fruit first to avoid it going off in the bowl.

As a guide the average man needs around 2,500 calories a day and the average woman 2,000. Make sure you have what you need on your plate at meal times, 3 times a day. (*NHS, 2013*).

The urge to nibble a work

Junk snacks and biscuits in my opinion are not as good at satisfying hunger as fruit, especially bananas and nuts, and are usually more expensive. Also generally the less natural a food is i.e. the more processed it is, it is going to have a greater impact on the planet in terms of reducing fuel consumption *Science Daily* (2008) and will therefore affect your secondary carbon footprint— the hidden impact which occurs in the manufacture and transportation of foods and products we buy. (*Encyclopaedia Britannica, 2013*)

Chips

Sliced potatoes sautéed or fried will be cheaper as you do not need to heat up the oven. They taste great and save you time too.

Meal times and protein

There can often be too much focus on what not to eat, and as a consequence you can lose sight of what your body needs to keep you happy and healthy.

The *BBC Science website* has a useful and concise page on the subject with a really helpful chart. As regards protein, it states you should eat two to three servings every day from

Meal times and protein *(continued)*

both plant and animal sources. One portion of protein could be meat or fish about the size of a standard pack of playing cards or one egg. *(BBC Science, 2013)*

Eat less meat and fish

Alternative sources of protein such as lentils and other pulses, nuts, beans and eggs are considerably cheaper than meat, so find out some suitable alternatives and give them a go. You could have a meat-free dinner more often each week or reduce the portion size of meat and have more non-meat protein alternatives added to the meal such as cottage pie with half mince/half adzuki beans. Go for quality not quantity. *Fruit and vegetables usually use much less water, energy and land to produce than meat, fish or processed foods unless locally sourced.*

Milk

Buy the largest size, and decant and freeze some if you need to. Remember a liquid will expand when frozen so make sure there is room for this in the bottle or remove a little before you freeze. PS – you can freeze yogurt too! *(Storingandfreezing.co.uk, 2013)* **Keep a few used 1 pint sized milk bottles ready to fill and store in the freezer for when you run out.**

Cheese

If you have to throw some cheese away occasionally, a few suggestions below that might help to minimize this.

Reduce the varieties you buy. You could buy a multi-purpose cheese, one that you can grate, eat and cook with.

If there is any mould on hard cheese be sure to remove it with a good measure of the surrounding cheese and discard.

Cheese
(continued)

The rest is fine to eat. To help your cheese not go mouldy so quickly add a sugar cube to the cheese cloche.

When grated cheese or soft cheese goes mouldy and that mould is not part of the cheese (like the blue in stilton) put all of it in the bin. This is not even suitable for cooking with.

You can also freeze cheese, Cheddar is ideal grated and frozen ready for cooking and a great time saver. Stilton works well in one piece too and we all buy too much of that at Christmas and do not know what to do with it. Other cheeses might lose their texture but taste the same. These may not be ideal for a dinner party but they're fine for everyday use and perfect for ensuring you have pre-grated cheese for cooking and sprinkling over things.

(Storingandfreezing.co.uk, 2013)

Bread

To avoid any bread going mouldy or stale, freeze what you will not use within 2 days. Sliced frozen bread can go straight in the toaster, for just a little longer than fresh bread.

Any type of bread is best kept at room temperature if not frozen. DO NOT put in the fridge. Fresh bread, rolls or baguettes keep fresh for longer if you keep them in their original wrapping or a plastic or paper bag. A paper bag keeps the bread mould free, but it can dry out quicker than a plastic bag. A plastic bag keeps bread softer but it is more likely to go mouldy as it can get too humid. If keeping for longer than 2 days put a few air holes in the plastic bag to reduce the chance of mould.

There is no need to buy breadcrumbs. Use any spare bread or rolls that have gone dry (not mouldy) to make your own breadcrumbs with either a rolling pin and a tray or the food mixer. Or you can use it to make deserts such as bread pudding.

Last night's baguette or bread, if kept in a plastic bag, can be sliced and toasted in the morning for breakfast or it can be brought back to life if you splash some water on it and reheat for a short time – eat it warm straight from the oven.

Biscuits

To use up biscuits, cook deserts with them as crumble toppings or use with breadcrumbs in savoury dishes with a twist.

To keep biscuits from going soft keep a sugar cube in the biscuit tin.

Measure food quantities

To avoid setting another place at the table for dinner for your pedal bin measure your food quantities when preparing dinner. You are less likely to have leftovers or waste food.

To help avoid leftovers, or to select the right quantity to freeze, measure out food portions and label x 1, 2, 3 or 4 as appropriate. A mix is useful to have in the freezer to cover all occasions.

The eatwell plate

Use the eatwell plate to help you get the balance right. It shows how much of what you eat should come from each food group

Group 1	Group 2	Group 3	Group 4	Group 5
Fruit and vegitables	Meat, fish, eggs, beans and other non-dairy sources of protein	Food and drinks high in fat and/or sugar	Milk and dairy foods	Bread, rice, potatoes, pasta and other starchy foods

© Crown Copyright 2013
Public Health England in association with the Welsh Government, the Scottish Government and the Food Standards Agency in Northern Ireland.

The recommended guide from the UK National Health Service is best described on their plate. As you can see

Measure food quantities
(continued)

you should be eating the same amount of fruit and/or vegetables as you do starchy food like bread, pasta, cereals, rice—roughly a third each on your plate, with the last third consisting mainly of meat and dairy and other proteins, with only a small amount of foods high in fat and sugar— biscuits, fizzy drinks, crisps. *(NHS, 2013)*

When preparing food I use the following rough guide per person: Starchy foods 100 grams cooked; that is about 2 medium potatoes, 60 grams uncooked pasta or 50 grams uncooked rice per person. Then about 100 grams of cooked vegetables, the more the merrier. I go for one whole vegetable per person i.e. a pepper or carrot and one for the pot. So in the end you have about a third of each on your plate and hopefully no waste and a balanced meal.

Defrosting food

Save energy by not using your microwave to defrost food.

Take frozen food out the night before you use it, or as soon as you know you need to defrost something for dinner, and put it in the fridge to defrost slowly. It is not ideal to leave food defrosting at room temperature as bacteria could form. All defrosted food should remain in the fridge and be cooked as soon as possible, preferably the same day. To speed defrosting up unpack and break the food up as best you can. Before you know it, it will be well on the way to being defrosted. Remember to keep food covered in the fridge at all times.

With frozen prawns cover them with cold tap water to very quickly defrost just before cooking.

For anything that has not quite defrosted in the fridge and you need for dinner, finish off defrosting in the microwave as you should not cook food that has not completely defrosted all the way through.

Use up the jars	Some tips if you want no wastage and no deteriorating pots of mayonnaise, nuts, gelatine etc. in your fridge or cupboards: Make a note of what needs to get used soon and bring it to the front or leave it on the kitchen worktop to remind you to use it. Find a way of incorporating it into your next meal. You can even get an app for this called *BigOven (2013)*.	
Make new dishes	Make new dishes out of uncooked leftovers to reduce food waste.	
Reuse Packaging	Re-use packaging you can't recycle. Use your old ice-cream tubs to freeze food in or as a compost kitchen caddy, or for storing other items such as sewing bits or bits and bobs in the garage for example. This will save you buying storage boxes.	

How to save when cooking

Principles

✓ Eat up what you have before buying more

✓ Use up the old before starting on the new

✓ Use your freezer

✓ Measure your portion sizes

Horrendous Household fact:

'In wealthy countries, about 210-250 pounds (95 to 115 kg) of food per capita is wasted annually, as fresh produce rots in the fridge, food is tossed after expiration dates, or left on the plate unconsumed. As a result, about 38 percent of global energy spent on food is wasted, says the United Nations' FAO.' (National Geographic, 2013).

The great thing about saving money while cooking is that it usually means saving time as well, so it is a win-win situation. You can get dinner on the table that little bit quicker and use less electricity in the process, and even better reduced washing up – always a plus! Here are some helpful hints to make the most of what you have instead of throwing it out straight away, as well as tips for what you can do without, saving you unnecessary clutter and of course money. I'm sure you do some of these things already without even thinking about it. Hopefully the list below will inspire you to try a few more ideas and take them on board.

| **Wash hands** | Wash hands before preparing food. Use the kitchen bowl to collect water rather than running a tap. | |

| **Oven and hob** | Set the temperature dial to the temperature you want and not higher (*it will not heat up any more quickly*). (*Affordable Warmth Network, 2013*) | |

Avoid opening the oven door while cooking. Turn off heat before you are finished as there is still some heat in the oven/hob, which will continue the cooking process.

When using the oven make the most of it and cook various dishes such as desserts and vegetables at the same time as well as the roast dinner. If you have a small upper-level oven, use that when you have smaller or fewer items.

Fan ovens use about 20% less electricity than conventional ovens. (*Affordable Warmth Network, 2013*)

| **Boil just enough** | Just boil enough water in the kettle for what you need, but remember to ensure the elements are covered with water. Most kettles can boil as little as a mugful. Measure how much water you need by filling your mug or saucepan with the required water and then pouring it into the kettle. | |

By only boiling what you need you could save £8 a year on energy bills. (*Energy Saving Trust, 2013*)

Remember to use the kettle water straight away once it's boiled to avoid boiling it again before you use it.

Use spare hot water wisely around the kitchen before it cools. Whenever you empty the kettle make it work - rinse the drainer, if hot, poor on weeds in the patio, use to clean or rinse dirty dishes.

When you buy your new kettle remember to get an energy-efficient one that can boil just one cup of water.

DID YOU KNOW

'In the UK three quarters of us overfill the kettle for our daily cuppa – costing Britain (all of us) a vast £68M a year!
(Energy Saving Trust, 2014)

Use your microwave

If you have a microwave it is a faster and more efficient way of cooking a variety of foods than an oven. *(Energy Saving Trust, 2013)*. Also, you can conveniently avoid frying or boiling food. Usually there's less washing up involved too.

Putting a microwaveable lid or upside down plate on your food helps retain moisture and reduces the potential clean-up if you have heated the food for too long.

Microwaves heat up the moisture in the food so if you overheat it, it will dry out and/or bubble over. When cooking meat, make sure it is cooked through as you would with any other method of cooking and check it is not too hot before serving.

How to boil things quickly

Use the kettle to boil the water first, then put only enough water in the pan to just cover the food and put the lid on. *(uswitch, 2014)* Once temperature has been reached turn down the heat to simmer.

Chopping food into smaller even pieces also ensures it cooks more quickly and requires less water.

Make sure the right pot is on the right spot. The base of your pots and pans should be flat and in contact with the heating surface. Ensure flames/heat are not visible around the pot. Use the smallest possible ring and pot when cooking.

Cleaning fruit and vegetables

When cleaning fruit and veg put the tap over a bowl so you collect the water and turn off the water when you have enough in the bowl. The remaining water can then go and be used to water the plants inside or out or pre-rinse dishes.

A hot pot

Always put a lid on your pots when cooking. (*uswitch, 2014*) You can use slightly less water this way and your food will cook more quickly at a lower temperature, as the heat is not lost and water does not evaporate.

Overcooking food

Overcooking your food—particularly your vegetables— will cost you not only more in energy bills but also in lost nutrients. *Institute for Optimum Nutrition (1992)*. How about microwaving or steaming your vegetables instead?

Steam cook

Use a steamer or steamer basket in your pot to use even less water, energy and time. This method of cooking reduces the loss of minerals and vitamins compared to boiling too. *Institute for Optimum Nutrition (1992)*.

Tea gone cold

Microwave a hot drink that has gone cold instead of throwing it away and making a new one. Twenty seconds usually does it and the drink will taste just the same.

Sugar in your tea

If you usually have a spoonful of sugar in your tea or coffee and you are having a cuppa with a biscuit or a piece of cake, you already are having much more than a spoonful of sugar already, so you might find you don't need that extra sugar in your drink. Why not give it a try? It works for me.

Toast

Use your toaster to make toast instead of the grill.

Pressure cooker

A pressure cooker or slow cooker is ideal for cooking stews, curries, red cabbage etc. The pressure cooker reduces the cooking time too for added convenience and reduced energy bills. Usually you use less water as well.

Cook in bulk

Cooking in bulk and freezing is a good way of saving time and energy. Ideal when you have more apples than you can eat from your garden or you want quick meals during the working week. Just freeze in portion sizes and label up so you know what it is.

Glass of water

You do not need to buy bottled water in a restaurant or to drink at home in the UK.

UK tap water is perfectly safe for drinking. It is also stringently tested and regulated, (*Water UK, 2013*) so for me it's the safer option. Saves money and unnecessary carrying too.

When getting water from the tap to drink do not let the tap run until it gets cold as this wastes perfectly good water too. Instead keep a jug of tap water in the fridge so it is ready to use, perfectly chilled, safe and tastes great. To ensure the water is always fresh use within 24 hours or empty out and fill up a fresh bottle each day. (*South West Water, 2013*).

With the old water from the jug you can fill your kettle or use as you would grey water to rinse before stacking the dishwasher or empty out on the plants etc.)

Glass of wine

Thanks to my sister in-law Sue for introducing me to all that saved wine.

To keep your wine fresh once you have opened the bottle. You can get a Vacuvin wine saver stopper or similar that takes all the air out of the bottle to keep it fresh for longer. (*Vacuvin, 2013*)

For sparkling wine or Champagne you can get a special stopper to keep the gas in and it really does work and makes the wine last for days.

Much better than the silver spoon trick

Cork

Remember cork comes from the bark of trees, so like wood it can go on the compost heap or in the compost bin. You can get plastic corks too now; they cannot be composted or recycled.

The metal wire around the sparkling wine cork can also be recycled, so save up all those bits and recycle in the metal skip at the recycling centre.

Freeze

If you have bought 500gms of meat and you only need 400gms, freeze the rest for another day or use the next day.

Freezer

Let cooked food cool down before putting it in the freezer.

An almost full freezer is a more efficient one, so stock up but do not overload. (*Which? 2014*)

Always keep the freezer door closed as much as possible and do not leave it open to get something to put in, even if for just for 30 seconds. It will use more energy to get the freezer back down to the correct temperature.

Running a freezer at a colder temperature than necessary will use more energy and therefore cost more to run. Freezers should be kept at -18°C to - 25°C. Use a fridge thermometer to ensure it is at the right temperature.

Fridge

Let cooked hot food cool down before putting in the fridge. Keep the fridge door closed as much as possible and do not leave open to get something to put in even for just 30 seconds, as above.

A full fridge is a more efficient one so stock up and put what you can in instead of in the larder such as opened sauce jars,

Fridge *(continued)*	eggs and vegetables, a jug of water etc. But do not overload. *(Affordable Warmth Network, 2013)*. Make sure the fridge is not too hot or cold with the aid of a thermometer. It should be no higher than +5°C. *(Food Standards Agency, 2015)*. If your fridge is too hot it will mean your food might spoil sooner or bacteria can form. If your fridge is too cold it will be working too hard and therefore using more electricity, and some of your food might partly freeze which is not ideal and might result in you having to bin/compost it.	
Empty pot and chopping boards	Make sure you don't waste any ingredients when preparing a meal by ensuring you empty the pot or chopping board totally. A rubber spatula is a great tool for getting that last bit out of pots too.	
Serving Food	Put food straight onto plates to save on extra washing up. If entertaining, use serving bowls to reduce wasting food as different people like different things and may not eat so much of some foods. That way you can freeze untouched leftovers easily.	
Leftovers	If you have a lot of leftovers you can use them up the next day by turning them into a new meal. If you have leftover meat for example you can make a cottage pie or pasta dish and perhaps add some adzuki or baked beans so you have enough for everyone. Leftover vegetables mix into a stew, curry or pie.	

Finish the last scrap

Only put food on the plates that you know will get eaten and then take more if you need it. (*For children put what they should eat on the plate, they can always get a second helping.*) This way any untouched leftovers can go in the fridge for someone to heat up in the microwave for their lunch or dinner the next day (*This is my usual lunch for one*).

If you are not going to use it within 2 – 3 days (*Food Standards Agency, 2015*), freeze and label so you know what it is. If in doubt freeze it rather than leaving it in the fridge for too long.

Totally empty

To get the rest out of a tube or pot, cut it open. Or you can remove the lid and let it drain onto a saucer. You'll find you can get another 1-2 servings out of a bottle, for example.

If using a bottled sauce, you can add a drop of boiling water into the jar or bottle, put the lid back on and shake and then all of it will pour out.

Mother nature

Grow your own fruit, veg and herbs if you can. This can be a lot of fun for all the family as well as saving you money and food miles. You don't need to have a garden; a patio, window box or windowsill can all be food production heaven and look pretty too. *For tips and ideas see links at the back of the book.*

A squeeze of lemon

To get more out of a fresh citrus such as lemons, dip the cut surface of the chilled fruit in a saucer of boiling water
(*Raymond Blanc, 2014*)

Peppers

No need to remove the pith, which is very sweet, just discard the seeds and stalk.

Mushrooms

Just clean and wipe; no need to peel or trim stalks.

Go bananas

You can use a ripe banana to aid tenderizing your joint, so if one has gone past its best the Sunday roast is the perfect place to use it up. (*Readers Digest, 2013*)

Go Raw

Eating raw food saves energy and water and also is good for you. Fruit and some vegetables, nuts and seeds make ideal snack foods.

Some packaging

You can use the packaging the food comes in to store things in the fridge or cupboard, and sometimes you can use this packaging to cook the food in. This saves on washing up and you get a little more use out of a plastic bag for example. So read the labels to see if you can save getting out the rubber gloves.

Paper Towels	No need for paper towels, use a kitchen cloth and add to your whites wash when necessary.	
Napkins	Wash your hands or use a linen table napkin instead of disposable paper napkins or towels and add to your whites wash.	
Cling film	In most cases you can do without cling film. For microwaving use an upside down bowl or plate instead. For the fridge or larder if you don't want to use an up-side-down plate you can also use another container instead, but decant any open cans. (*NHS, 2013*) You can use an old biscuit tin for pastries in the larder.	
Kitchen foil	In most cases there is no need for kitchen foil. Jacket potatoes cook best and quickest in the microwave, so no foil is needed. Put the roast in a pot with a lid instead. Then remove the lid around 30 minutes before cooking time is complete to brown. Put your meat on a wire rack and put water in the baking tray below instead of silver foil to catch the fat which drips down, keep adding water as needed if it evaporates. Once you have finished cooking, tip the fat and water mixture down the sink with left over boiled kettle water or put in your green cone once cooled. For more info on a green cone, see garden section. If you are cooking duck or goose save the fat juices. Just tip into an old jam jar and let it cool before storing in the fridge ready for use. Great for basting roast potatoes etc.	

Freezer bags

No need to buy freezer bags. Use various plastic bags (or plastic containers) for freezing food.

Only use a bag which contained food to freeze food. For example reuse bread bags to freeze bread if not using within 2 days. Frozen vegetable bags are useful to freeze leftover soup. Use old spaghetti bags can hold two chicken breasts or a small leftover. Rinse bags first and turn inside out to dry if needed. Larger bags such as pasta bags or fajita bags can be used for any food you want to freeze raw or pre-cooked.

For food hygiene and safety reasons I don't reuse any bags that had cooked or uncooked meat or fish in them. I keep all the bags I get in all shapes and sizes, and I always have plenty so I reuse once for the freezer and then downgrade *(see tip below)*.

The NHS guide on how to store food safely states 'With more and more people re-using carrier bags ... re-useable bags (and single-use carrier bags) should be disposed of if there are spillages of raw meat juices.' *(NHS, 2013)*

Plastic tubs

You don't need to buy plastic tubs, you can use your old ice-cream tub to freeze liquids like soup or apple compote, or some leftover dinner. *See hygiene details above.*

Reuse your plastic bags

There is no need to buy any type of plastic bags. Keep and reuse plastic bags of all shapes and sizes. Store in a drawer in the kitchen and use as needed.

Once you have reused a bag for freezing, downgrade it, for example by using it as a peelings bag for compost or a poo bag for pets. With bags that had cooked or uncooked meat or fish in it, throw them away or use them as poo bags only.

Any old plastic bags are also ideal as bin liners around the house and kitchen.

Matches - reuse

Put used matches back in the box the other way round and use the other end when you can. This way you only ever need to use one new match at any one time *(to light the first candle)*. Thereafter use the used matches to light everything else from that candle. This is especially useful to remember around Christmas time when candles around the house create a wonderful festive feel. Put used matches in the kitchen home composting container instead of the bin when used up.

A tip I picked up from my husband.

Kitchen recycling made easy

Put the compost bin caddy in the most convenient place and put the pedal bin as far away as possible. That way everyone else in the house—including teenagers!—will pick the nearest if they can. Sneaky I know!

Have a recycling box next to the pedal bin that way cans, bottles can go straight into the right box.

Rinse containers if needed. If rinsing, you can use 'grey' water from your washing up bowl or from the water butt, instead of drinking water from the tap.

What to do with your peelings

Collect kitchen peelings in an old ice cream pot or kitchen caddy lined with an old plastic bag and start a compost heap in the garden. You can add coffee grounds and teabags too, as well as all uncooked fruit and veg. See garden section for more details.

Organic matter in a landfill produces *methane*, which is about 21 times more potent a greenhouse gas than *carbon dioxide*, so composting is really worth doing. You also end up with free compost for your garden, hanging baskets etc.

Green Cone

Collect all food scraps cooked and uncooked, mouldy or not, such as raw meat trimmings, bones, flour, bread, food scraps from plates, sinks and worktops, Any food that you would not put on the compost heap can all go in a green cone. You can also include uncooked fruit and vegetables too if you want. See garden section for more details.

If you have a local council food waste collection you can use that instead for all your food scraps and still have a compost heap for the rest if you wish.

Recycling

You can recycle various things from the kitchen. The main ones are food waste, glass bottles and jars, paper and card, food and drink cans, plastic bottles. Egg boxes can go on the compost heap, which is ideal if your garden is mainly lawn, or you can recycle them with the cardboard. Some areas take aluminium foil, textiles and old small electrical items too.

How to save when cleaning

Principles

✓ No need for harsh chemicals

✓ Only squeeze what you need – less is more

✓ Use up the old before starting on the new

✓ Elbow grease is the cheapest and greenest way to clean

Horrendous Household fact:

'70% of the Earth is covered with water but only about 1% of the world's water is readily available for human use. Nearly 97% is salty or otherwise undrinkable. Another 2% is locked in the ice caps and glaciers. That leaves just 1% for all humanity's needs.' (Waterwise, 2013).

I hate cleaning, but at the same time I hate mess and dirt in the house; so for me it is all about getting it done properly, safely and all importantly, quickly. Prevention is better than cure and takes the grind out of cleaning as little and often is great as you don't get bored or worn out.

Another pet hate for me is carrying an array of chemical potions up and down the stairs. By cutting it down to a few simple basics I think I have saved loads of effort, unless I'm practicing for a half marathon! The great thing about less cleaning stuff is that you save money too, and there's less indoor pollution from chemicals in the home (*The Royal Borough of Kensington and Chelsea, 2013*). Remember in this instance less always gives you more.

Below are a few ideas I have I picked up that hopefully you will find useful—especially, if like me, you have eczema and asthma.

Grey Water in the kitchen

'Grey' water is water you have used once already. It is not 100% clean but it's still useful. If you use it when you can, this saves using fresh drinking water from the tap. For example put left over tap water from used drinking glasses onto the plants or into your watering can or add to the washing up bowl when just rinsing dishes before stacking the dishwasher. There are various suggestions throughout the book and perhaps you can think of a few more for yourself.

Plug in or bowl up!

For minimal water use always ensure the plug is in before you start or use a washing up bowl. You could reduce water wastage by 50% (*Waterwise, 2014*).

This is also good for spotting small leaks and the water collected can be used for watering plants or rinsing your dishes.

Rinsing dishes

Use grey water to rinse dishes before stacking the dishwasher or for soaking before draining the sink and filling with fresh hot soapy water to do the dishes. You will need less washing up liquid as well this way.

Washing up

Do the washing up when you have enough or at the end of the day, so you only need to use one full bowl and you only have to wash up once. Clean glasses first and leave the dirtiest till last to make the bubbles and water last longer.

The Energy Saving Trust states 'Using a sink of water to wash up twice a day rather than having the hot tap running could save around £34 a year on your gas bill and around £25 on your water bill.' (*Energy Saving Trust, 2013*). If you need to rinse utensils or wash vegetables, use cold water if possible, collect it in the bowl and avoid leaving the tap running.

Collecting water

When rinsing a mug before making another cup of tea, when washing vegetables or rinsing a plate before stacking the dishwasher, do it over a bowl in the sink or put the plug in the sink and collect the water. Turn off the tap as soon as you have enough water or if you need to use the bowl.

After a while you don't need to turn the tap on to rinse dishes, just use this 'grey' water and then stack the dishwasher or put the dish to one side to wash up in clean hot soapy water later.

If you don't have a dishwasher, rinsing dirty plates as above in this way saves work, water, energy and time.

Worktops

No need for extra sprays and products. It is perfectly safe to use hot soapy water with a clean dishcloth, and it's sensible to do this every time before and after preparing food. (*NHS, 2013*) Soda crystals are very good at cutting through grease so also ideal for a weekly clean of the kitchen surfaces and rinse and dry off.

Also you can use a mixture of bicarbonate of soda with water, rinse and dry off.

I find soda crystals the most effective as well as cost effective, especially for grease.

Cleaning cloths

To ensure that your cloths are clean wash them regularly and ensure they are dry before you use them again. (NHS, 2013)

I also like to soak mine on its own in the washing up bowl and pour left over boiled water from the kettle over it from time to time.

Buy cloths you can use again and again instead of disposable cloths and sponges – or heaven forbid paper towels – and wash them in the washing machine along with your darks. Downgrade your cloths once they are past their best for the washing up, for example for bathroom cleaning and last of

Cleaning cloths
(continued)

all toilet cleaning. Wash regularly and if you wish like me boil occasionally too.

Try eco-friendly cloths such as E-Cloths that you can reuse and do not need any cleaning products to clean with for around the home. They remove dirt, grease and over 99% of bacteria with just water! In fact you can't use cleaning products with them, as you will see on the instructions. This saves on clutter and chemicals as well as pounds saved! *(EnviroProducts Ltd, 2013)*

Keep things clean with bicarbonate of soda

The cleaner your cooking appliances are the more energy efficient they will be. Also they are less likely to smoke out the kitchen requiring urgent action in the form of opening doors and windows letting out all that heat you paid for. It'll stop the fire alarm going off too!

Bicarbonate of soda with a little water cleans most things brilliantly; plastic, porcelain, chrome, glass, stainless steel (scrub along the grain) and silverware.

Just dab some on a damp cloth and use as you would any cream cleaner. It also deodorizes at the same time. *(Dri-Pak Ltd, 2014)*

Wonderful on tea stains too!

DO NOT USE BICARBONDATE OF SODA ON ALUMINIUM, seek manufacturer's instructions.

Oven

Instead of those potentially polluting chemicals try the green and pleasant variety of cleaners. There are loads of options that work but of course it depends on how baked on the stains are. The most common ingredients are bicarbonate of soda, salt, water, vinegar and lemon juice. These can be used in different quantities and combinations and they are all effective.

For really burnt-on food, which has gone black or carbonised, mix equal parts salt and bicarbonate of soda

Oven
(continued)

and add vinegar and let it fizz for a while in a cold oven.

Go back to the oven after a while and scrub. This is also great for the burnt-on food in pots and pans.

I also like to use wire wool for burnt on oven stains especially for the odd speck.

Repeat as needed or leave to soak overnight.

You could also try a daily routine of spraying the carbon deposits in the oven with a solution of 3 teaspoons of bicarbonate of soda mixed with tap water in a new spray bottle. The bicarbonate of soda only works when damp so keep spraying every so often, repeat and leave as long as possible before wiping away with a damp cloth. If needed repeat and leave for longer. (*Guildford Cleaning Company, 2014*). (*I do this with an old spray bottle I have rinsed with a dash of boiling water and swished around a few times, to ensure there is no residues of any kind. To check there is no residue, put some tap water in the bottle and shake. If you have some bubbles there is still residue so repeat*).

Hob

It is best to have the kitchen cloth handy when cooking so you can wipe away spillages. For every day, warm soapy water is fine.

With burnt-on food, prevention is better than cure. Once dried on, a hob scraper for ceramic hobs is also a handy chemical-free solution, which is quick to use. Wipe or scrape away any thick bits first. My favourite way is to sprinkle on a teaspoon of soda crystals and use a clean damp cloth. It removes grease and burnt on food too. Rinse with water and give a final dry wipe with your e-cloth.

Even though the method above is quicker and cheaper you might want to make your own green and pleasant-smelling alternative to those chemicals under the sink. If so, you could make a paste from bicarbonate of soda, lemon juice if you have spare (if not vinegar) and a bit of warm water. Use with a damp cloth as needed.

Cut down on pots

Save on washing up. Sometimes you can cook things in the same pot together or use the pot again, the same goes for bowls and plates too, so think about how you can make your meal preparation more efficient.

If you are like me I will really rack my brains to think of a way to create less washing up.

Rinsing in 'grey water' as you go really helps too.

Microwave

Clean microwaves with warm soapy water.

If you need to remove hard, dried-on food use elbow grease but as with the hob and oven, prevention is better than cure, so wipe as you go. If that does not appeal you can create steam in your microwave to aid loosening the burnt on food by heating tap water. Some people add vinegar due to its deodorising abilities. Pour about a cup of water and some vinegar into a bowl and place in the microwave, heat on full power until boiling (approximately 2 minutes) and then leave to cool down.

Wipe surfaces with a cloth and some bicarbonate of soda to help remove stubborn bits. (Which? 2014)

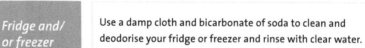

Fridge and/ or freezer

Use a damp cloth and bicarbonate of soda to clean and deodorise your fridge or freezer and rinse with clear water.

To keep your fridge smelling fresh keep a small tub of bicarbonate of soda, as it is an excellent deodoriser, in the fridge with the lid off. Mix from time to time. Replace every couple of months or so and then use to clean elsewhere in the house. (Dri-Pak Ltd, 2014)

Kettle water

Don't fill the kettle up, just use the amount of water you need. If you have some reasonably hot water left use this for cleaning the dishes before topping up with hot water from the tap. Use left over hot water to clean around sink instead of turning the tap on or use to pour on weeds in the patio, instead of weed killer.

Lime scale

For chrome and kettles, sink plugholes and other kitchen metal surfaces, the most effective and natural way is vinegar. You can also use lemon juice but I tend to stick with vinegar because I think it's cheaper and more effective. It gives a brilliant shine to all metals and you can wipe it away with a clean damp cloth. No need for another type of cleaner or de-scaler. Kettles work more efficiently when not scaled up, and tea tastes better too. If necessary leave the kettle to soak for an hour. Reuse the vinegar for other cleaning jobs around the sink and store in an old glass jar (remember to label it!)

Instead of buying vinegar to clean your metal surfaces, don't throw out your jars of pickle. Once you have finished the pickled onions or gherkins, put the liquid-filled jars under the kitchen sink with the rest of the cleaning products and use when needed.

To clean the chrome sink plughole, first put the plug in and pour on vinegar until the area is covered. Leave for a few minutes until removed or rub off gently with a cloth or old toothbrush.

Soda crystals are ideal for de-scaling too. Use them on tiles, flooring and even your coffee machine every now and then to help keep it in good working order. Add them to the water and run through the machine and then repeat with clean water twice to rinse before using for coffee. (*Mistral Lab Supplies, 2014*)

Use less product – less is more!

Use just what you need so you don't waste anything. A good rule is that once you have squeezed it out you have to wear it out. This means you are either cleaning the kitchen surfaces and the microwave as well as the dishes or you remember to squeeze only what you need for the washing up. The same goes for cleaning brass, silver and the kitchen floor.

Washing up liquid

Buy concentrated whenever you can, you can add water at home if you wish or use less as instructed with every squirt. *(The same applies for all cleaning detergents)*.

If washing up by hand clean glasses first and leave the dirtiest till last to make the bubbles and water last longer. Don't forget to squirt the washing-up liquid into the bowl first, then add the water and use a brush to whip into lather. That way you use less detergent. It is easy to squirt too much liquid; if you have bubbles left over in your wash use less next time. Or top up the washing up liquid bottle with water to dilute the liquid if you prefer; whatever works for you.

An alternative for washing up liquid if you are heavy handed, is to add water to the bottle to dilute it so you don't waste so much.

Alternatively, get a washing up brush where you add washing up liquid into the handle. It's convenient and does the job as a little comes out at a time when you use it – my current favourite.

Always buy concentrated - just remember to use less.

Tea stains

Avoid using chemicals, instead wipe with a damp cloth and salt if needed or bicarbonate of soda if you prefer.

Finish the last scrap	Cut open the tube or pot to get the rest out too. Or you can remove the lid and let it drain onto a saucer or the draining board. Saves money by getting another 1-2 washing up bowls out of a bottle for example.	
Organise	Ensure you put new supplies at the back of the cupboard next to the current opened one. This goes for anything from more toilet rolls and shoe polish to cleaning chemicals. The longer things are lying around the higher the chance they can get damaged, go off or lose their appeal. Use up all of the old before you start on the new.	
Dishwasher	Stack the dishwasher to the full before putting it on. If there is no burnt-on food or if it's been pre rinsed-in the sink use a lower setting, which skips pre-rinsing it again. Saves time, energy and wear on your dishwasher. 'Dishwashers can take up a significant chunk of your electricity bill, costing on average around £47 a year to run. Over a year, it costs around £7 less to run an Energy Saving Trust Recommended dishwasher than it does an old, inefficient machine – and it will use less water.' (*Energy Saving Trust, 2013*) To descale your dishwasher you can use white vinegar. For best results Dri-pak suggest filling ... 'two containers on the top and bottom rack and to set the dishwasher on the longest, hottest wash.' (*Dri-Pak Ltd, 2014*) If you need to deodorize your dishwasher you can also sprinkle some bicarbonate of soda onto the bottom underneath the dish racks.	

| **Glass** | When glass starts to look cloudy and past its best you can get it looking like new by cleaning with bicarbonate of soda on a damp cloth. Great for water jugs, ashtrays and glasses that have been in the dishwasher a lot. A quick and easy wipe is all that is needed. | |

| **Non - stick coating** | To extend the life of your non-stick frying pans the key is to avoid scratching the coating. Only use soft plastic utensils with a light touch when cooking. | |

Wash with a cloth as gently as possible and do not put in the dishwasher. Avoid any tiny scratches you can't see, they all build up over time and before you know it the pan is ruined and looks terrible. Reducing the heat on these pans when cooking helps to make cleaning easier and saves energy too.

If you wish you can buy alternatives. They may be more expensive to buy, but in the long run it might suit you better. There are also 'green' non-stick alternatives. One such supplier is the GreenPan company, details at the back of the book.

Bathroom

Principles

✓ Fresh air is best

✓ Less is more

Horrendous Household fact:

'Did you know that only 4% of the perfectly drinkable water you use every day is used for drinking? Or, that nearly a third of the water used in your home, is literally flushed down the toilet? What a waste!' (Waterwise, 2013).

The bathroom is one of those places that you never seem to have enough storage space for all those potions and lotions, so using up what you have saves space, helps cash-flow and makes it easier to clean the bathroom too.

Clearly you can waste a lot of water, and don't forget energy as well, as most of it will be in the form of hot water too. You will be surprised how it all adds up.

Turn the tap off

Do not leave the tap running while cleaning your teeth.

OFWAT, the government regulator of the water industry in England and Wales states 'A running tap uses up to nine litres of water a minute. (*OFWAT, 2014*)

'A dripping hot water tap wastes energy and in one week wastes enough hot water to fill half a bath...' (*Energy Saving Trust, 2014*)

Fix the tap

Fix any leaks as soon as possible. it could save you over £18 a year! (Waterwise, 2014). In the meantime collect the water in a bowl, watering can or kettle until the leak, however small, is fixed. You will be surprised how much you collect.

'A dripping tap can waste more than 60 litres of water per week. In most cases, all that is required is a new washer'. (*Thames Water, 2014*)

Banish the bath

No need to use the bath, use the shower instead.

OFWAT states 'A five-minute shower uses about 40 litres of water. This is about half the volume of a standard bath.' (*OFWAT, 2014*)

'If everybody in your family of four replaces one bath a week with a five minute shower, you can save up to £15 a year on gas bills and up to £25 on water bills (if you have a water meter). (*Energy Saving Trust, 2014*)

Shower

Avoid running the taps or a showerhead while waiting for the hot water for your shower. If you must, at the very least don't turn on the shower until you are in there and hold the shower in your hand away from you. Then turn it on and wait until it is hot enough for you. Every second counts and a minute of wasted water costs you energy and water bills.

Remember to turn the tap off too while shampooing, applying soap, etc. If you don't want to do that, wash your

Shower
(continued)

hair separately, bending over the bath/shower tray and turning the water off in between applying shampoo.

'On average a shower uses 10 litres of water a minute.'

(Thames Water, 2014)

Heads up for showers

Replacing your showerhead with an efficient one could save you around £75 a year off your gas bill for a typical family of 4 and around £90 off your water bill each year. If you have a water meter, that's £165! *(Energy Saving Trust, 2014)*

There are various options on the market, and they can halve your shower water consumption but enhance the shower feel by sucking in air for a gorgeous luxury feel. Of course the less water you use the less energy you use to heat it. Suitable for power showers without reduced performance, but not suitable for electric showers.

Go for cold

Which tap you turn on at the sink is more of a habit most of the time than a conscious thought. So to avoid wasting energy check you automatically go for the cold tap (unless you need hot water) or make a conscious effort to switch to cold as a general rule, when you can. If you are turning the tap on for only a couple of seconds, the hot water will not reach you in that short space of time so go for cold instead.

Unblock it

If you need to unblock your shower, bath, sink or drain, before you grab for another bottle off the supermarket shelf try this simple and easy solution: Remove any visible bits and pull out any trays you can. Use a plunger if you have one. If not shake in about one to two tablespoons of bicarbonate of soda down the plug then add a whoosh of vinegar. *(How stuff works, 2014)* It will fizz for a bit, so leave for a while. Rinse with hot (not boiling)

Unblock it
(continued)

water to check it is unblocked. Remove any visible lumps of hair if you see them. Repeat as needed. If all else fails, buy a plunger. You can also use soda crystals too.

Prevention is better than cure so use a simple drain sieve, which cost around a £1 each and cuts out the hassle of hair blocking up the drain. Hair can go into your compost bin in the kitchen. Also poor left over hot water [NOT BOILING] down your drain once a week. (*How stuff works, 2014*)

Whoosh is my technical term for about a cup

Toilet flushing

You can further reduce the water you use by not flushing every time you go—if it's yellow let it mellow. This can easily be done at night so as not to wake the house, and/or apply to the upstairs toilet only, asking visitors to use the downstairs loo instead.

'On average, each flush uses 7 litres of water.'
(*Thames Water, 2014*)

Water hippo

A water hippo or similar (1 litre tub or bag) reduces water used for each flush by 1 litre. You can make your own by using an old ice cream tub. Put something in it like a large pebble to make sure it stays at the bottom of the cistern. Put the lid on (i.e. no water in the ice cream tub) and then submerge in the toilet cistern, where it will not interfere with the flushing lever. You need to be able to flush and allow the lever to come back so it does not constantly flush. It does not require any DIY skills but if you are not sure how to do it, seek advice first. Not suitable for toilets that have a cistern below 6 litres.

You could save between one and three litres each time you flush the toilet with a water saving device. (*OFWAT, 2014*)

Your local water company might provide you a save-a-flush bag for free, so visit their website to find out what is on offer.

All steamed up

Instead of an extractor fan just open the window to prevent steaming up.

It is important to air the house and let fresh air in. Good ventilation can also limit moisture. 'Damp indoor spaces foster the growth and transmission of viruses and bacteria. Controlling moisture indoors can limit the spread of these infectious diseases and also limit mould...' (*American Lung Association, 2013*).

Relevant not just for the bathroom, but perhaps your dampest room in the house. Of note, it is worth bearing in mind that aerosols can provide a food source for moulds, so banish them where you can. (*Anglian Water Services, 2013*)

Sink

Always put the plug in before you use the sink. That way you are using every drop of water and wasting nothing. Turn off the water as soon as you have enough in the sink to wash your face or hands.

Any grey water in the sink when you are finished could be used to water plants upstairs for example.

Sparkling clean

Cutting down on the amount of cleaning products in the house is more convenient as well as more economical. For a greener way, all you need in the house is vinegar, bicarbonate of soda and salt.

This is not only greener but cheaper and easier too. Use vinegar on all chrome and enamel. For stubborn lime scale leave a bit of vinegar to cover the plughole in the sink for a few minutes, then rinse and wipe dry with an eco-cloth to finish. If you still have any lime scale scrub with a toothbrush and add a bit of bicarbonate of soda. If it's really bad cover with vinegar and add a teaspoon of bicarbonate of soda, let it fizz then scrub as usual.

For sensitive tiles or surfaces just use bicarbonate of soda with a little water.

Sparkling clean
(continued)

From trials I have done even on PVC window frames and doors the results are the same whether you use bicarbonate of soda or a cream cleaner. Stubborn marks are best removed with an old toothbrush or scrubbing brush to loosen the mark and is a lot quicker than adding more cleaning fluid. Elbow grease is quicker and better and of course cheaper.

Vinegar is more effective than any lime scale remover I have ever tested!

Cleaning teeth and Tooth - brushes

Remember to put the plug in the sink before you start cleaning your teeth. Turn the tap off after you have rinsed your toothbrush. Don't keep the tap running. Use a glass if you want to rinse your mouth afterwards with water.

You can clean your toothbrush by putting it into a glass of water with two teaspoons of bicarbonate of soda. Let it soak overnight. (*The Children's Oral Health Institute, Maryland, 2014*)

Save your old toothbrushes. They are the perfect cleaning tools for all those hard to reach places in the home.

Toothpaste

Once you have squeezed out all you can, cut the tube open and use up the rest. Scooping out a bit at a time will give you 3 or 4 extra cleans.

A good rule is that once you have squeezed it out you have to wear it out. This means either cleaning your teeth for a very long time or remembering to squeeze out only a pea-sized amount.

If you run out of toothpaste you can make your own by mixing bicarbonate of soda with a little water and brushing as usual. This will remove stains, so you can use once a week if you need to. (*Readers Digest, 2014*)

Cardboard packaging around toothpaste is no use, so buy toothpaste without it if you can, or leave in the supermarket if you dare. Otherwise recycle the card box with your paper.

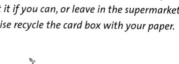

Extra uses for toothpaste

A tip for cold sores, try a dab of toothpaste. What Allergy seems to agree. (*What Allergy? 2014*)

Use the clear variety if you can, that way no one knows you have it on. It dries the cold sore out and seals it in to stop it spreading. Put it on as soon as it possible and leave it on. Put a barrier cream around the rest of the mouth for added protection to stop it spreading and keep your lips soft.

Amazing!

Toilet cleaner

For everything above the water line use vinegar and if you wish add a little bicarbonate of soda. For cleaning below the water line add about a cup of vinegar in the toilet and then add about a tablespoon of bicarbonate of soda. You will see it fizz; ideally leave it to do its thing while cleaning the rest of the bathroom. This is just as effective as using thick bleach.

As you know, the key to a clean toilet is removing the lime scale, as the dirt will stick to it and is unsightly. Sometimes, no matter how many chemicals or green alternatives you use, you'll need to scrub to remove the lime scale. A weekly cleaning thereafter will save on elbow grease.

Once the toilet is in hand, you can use salt instead of bicarbonate of Soda to scrub with vinegar and flush away.

Mouthwash

This should not be used to clean your teeth. Just use toothpaste and a toothbrush.

If you do have mouthwash, use it when you are not cleaning your teeth to freshen breath after a meal or at other times of the day. Alternatively just use tap water, as the gargling action helps rinse your teeth, or eat an apple after your meal and get one of your five a day at the same time.

My dentist advised not to use mouthwash straight after cleaning my teeth, and the NHS seem to agree. It washes away some of the benefits of the toothpaste. (*NHS, 2013*)

Mouthwash *(continued)*	To make your own mouthwash take half a teaspoon of bicarbonate of soda and half a glass of water *(Dr Peterson, 2014)*. Use, as you would mouth wash, gargle and spit out. This mixture also soothes heartburn; just swallow instead *(NHS, 2014)*.	

Turn off the standbys	Do not keep items on standby; they still use energy, however little. Once charged pull out the plug of the electric toothbrush *(Colgate-Palmolive (UK) Limited, 2013)*.	

Toilet paper	For use while on the toilet only. No need to use for anything else such as blowing your nose or wiping your glasses, see suggestions below. Buy recycled and non-bleached toilet paper. There is definitely no need for moist toilet paper or wipes; it is no substitute for washing.	

Handkerchiefs	Use material handkerchiefs instead of paper ones or toilet paper for blowing your nose, wiping your glasses etc. Wash handkerchiefs with whites. For those with allergies like me, it helps to stop you sneezing. If you have a cold you need to consider putting the used one in the wash basket and getting a new one so that you do not spread the bacteria around. Or for a short period use toilet paper. You need to make a judgment at the time as to what is best - a sorer nose or trying to reduce the spread of the cold.	

Air fresheners

*A pet hate of mine
as they can contain
formaldehyde.*

No need for air fresheners; just open a window.

Keep perfumes in the bathroom and or downstairs cloakroom or toilet; so when you put some on, it helps keep the room smelling fresh too.

Use up old perfume/deodorant sprays if you want to mask an odour (like the dog bed). Once empty do not replace.

Vinegar and bicarbonate of soda are natural products that absorb odours.

In a room an open jar of vinegar works well as does bicarbonate of soda. You can also sprinkle a bit on the dog bed.

Cotton wool

There is no need for cotton wool. Try to use less of it.

To remove makeup from the whole face use a squirt of your cleanser or makeup remover and apply with your hands on damp skin then rinse off. Best leave eyes until last as this is where you will need to reapply if not all mascara is removed.

Best of all use a microfibre face cloth; this is very effective at removing any leftover mascara and make up and you need never buy cotton wool again. Wash the cloth with whites or colours and remember not to use fabric softener with microfibre cloths.

Soap is best

Use soap instead of liquid washes such as shower gel. Soap lasts longer and is usually cheaper too so it will save you money. There is almost no wastage and minimal packaging. Once the soap bar is too small to hold, squash onto a new one. Less clutter In the bathroom too.

With shower gels you are paying for the water they dilute the soap with as well as the bottle, and of course you are carrying a much heavier product home that can spill and break.

Beats me why it ever caught on and we all started to buy it

Wet-wipes, moist lets, baby-wipes	There is no need to buy these 'use once throw away' products, instead use a damp flannel. Less chemicals on the skin too, always a good thing.	
Cosmetics	Cosmetics can range from cheap to eye-wateringly expensive, whether it's lipstick and other makeup to moisturizers, eye creams and so on. The key is to buy the less harsh chemical varieties, which will be kinder to your skin and the planet. There are various ethical brands out there that bring together the desire to provide more natural and organic products. These products are usually less likely to have animal testing and reduce their carbon emissions from packaging choices to production techniques.	
Use less product	Use just what you need so you don't waste any product. Also cut open to get the rest out. Saves money by getting another 1-2 more applications of body lotion out of a bottle of moisturizer for example. To keep fresh, cut across the middle of the soft bottle/tube and bend one and push the other on top, if you like things tidy like me.	
Skin irritations	A product to have in the bathroom, which you might have guessed by now, is bicarbonate of soda. It soothes a variety of skin irritations, from adding two tablespoons or so to your bath (*Channel 4, 2014*); to mixing a paste with water for bites, sunburn and for bee stings. (*Dri-Pak Ltd, 2014*)	
Tea tree oil	Can be used on mildew and mould. I recommend using cheaper green alternatives like vinegar and bicarbonate of soda if you can, though. But I still have it in my bathroom cupboard as it is an alternative beauty product for a host of minor aliments so I have included it.	

Potions and lotions

Use up and finish what you have before you open the next pot and/or buy another. This is a simple but a very effective way of saving money and improving your cash flow. Why have money sitting in your shelves for months waiting to be used when it can be earning you interest in the bank or building society. Less stuff means less time doing housework too.

Don't like a cream

If you don't like a cream that you use for your face any more, maybe you think it doesn't agree with you, you don't need to throw it in the bin. Whatever the cream, just use it up as a body lotion or hand cream. This works for anything from eye cream to sun tan lotion. Just use up the leftovers and get them out of the way.

Natural creams

Instead of buying creams from the beauty counter you can opt for the more natural ones from your fridge or larder. Also worth remembering if you run out.

Here are a few I have discovered along the way that I have tested mysel f– along with where I found the information. You will find many sources on the web that agree: almond oil for a rich hair conditioner for super soft hair. (*Beena's Beauty Clinic, 2009*)

Margarine as a makeup remover. In fact any oil such as baby oil will work. (*A tip from a former model*). Just use what suits your skin and remember to cleanse afterwards to remove any excessive oil as you would usually do with cosmetic alternatives.

Avocado oil to soften hard skin on feet. Not only is it cheaper, it's a must in summer when wearing flip-flops to avoid/repair cracked heals. (Beena's Beauty Clinic, 2014) Avocado is also an all-round good moisturiser with lots of beneficial properties (*Med-Health, 2014*).

Natural creams
(continued)

You might want to experiment and mix your own face cream and body lotion to suit you. It's as easy as making mayonnaise.

There are plenty of options and ideas around so search online or get a book out from the library. Make small amounts and ideally store in the fridge. Homemade creams, like food, will not contain any preservatives so you can't leave them in the cupboard for months.

Deodorant

If you run out of deodorant or you want a more natural alternative, take a little bicarbonate of soda in your hand and pat on under your armpit. *(Readers Digest, 2014)*

Nail varnish remover

Use nail varnish remover by adding a few drops to nail varnish that is getting too thick, then shake with lid on and apply as usual. This helps you get the most out of your old nail varnish.

If you need to remove your nail varnish, especially useful if removing gels or shellac, soak your nails in a small bowl and when ready remove with an old face cloth or similar that you keep just to remove nail varnish. This saves time and there's no need to buy cotton wool any more.

Instead of throwing away the remaining nail varnish, tip back in to an old bottle and leave the sediment behind and bin it. Reuse this used nail varnish first before adding more nail varnish remover.

Ideally keep an old nail varnish remover bottle for this, or use a small thick plastic bottle made of HDPE for example. (Do not use a thin plastic bottle, like an old water bottle. This is not suitable to contain a strong chemical, like nail varnish remover).

Samples

Save skin care and other samples for when you go on holiday or stay overnight away from home at a friend's or in a hotel. Even if they aren't your usual brand it is always worth using as you could find a new favourite. So give them a go when you want to travel light.

You can use a face cream sample as a body lotion if you wish too if you prefer. If you are not expecting to go away over the next 12 months, use up these tiny tubes first as they can dry out, especially airplane toothpaste.

Hotel stuff

Bring home any half used soaps, shampoos etc. and finish off. The hotel will more than likely just bin them, which is a waste. The pots might also be really handy to use to fill up with your normal brand of shampoo or moisturizer for when you want to travel light for an overnight stop, when visiting family, to take to the gym or on a short break holiday.

Towels

The fewer towels in use at any one time, the less washing needed. You can put all other whites in the same wash. This way it may be possible to wash your towels more often without the need of a separate wash.

Cotton buds

You can cut down on their use by using a microfiber cloth instead to wipe away bits of makeup or mascara instead of cotton buds or toilet paper.

Likewise to clean your ears instead of using a cotton bud use the corner area of your towel or face cloth before it goes in the wash. In fact you should avoid using cotton buds to clean your ears. (*Net Doctor, 2013*)

Sanitary products

'More than 4 million tampons and pads are flushed away a day in the UK [alone] ...' (*Women's Environmental Network, 2004*) So how can we reduce this?

Firstly tampons etc. are best put in the bin instead of flushed down the toilet for all sorts of reasons, so please try to remember to do that.

The easy way to reduce this burden on the environment and save money is to swap to sanitary towels most of the time to start with; you will probably use fewer this way. Try to buy non-chlorine bleached varieties.

You can also buy various reusable options online, and the Women's Environmental Network has a useful fact sheet. You'll find details on menstrual cups and washable panty liners, which you can get from various suppliers online like Honour Your Flow, from Cumbria. See link at the back of the book.

Hairdryer

You can cut down on how much you use the hairdryer. After washing your hair, towel dry as much as possible and comb through. Then do all the other things you want to do before going out, including your makeup. This allows the hair to partly dry naturally, meaning reduced time drying your hair and less electricity used. Also less heat equals fewer split ends and therefore fewer trips to the hairdresser, which will save you even more money.

This saves loads of time, especially if you have long hair like me.

Combs

Clean combs and brushes with a little shampoo or let them soak in the sink with a little water. Alternatively you can use a little bicarbonate of soda instead.

Razors

Disposable razors are not ideal because you keep buying the same thing again and again.

Buy reusable ones instead if you can.

Ladies, avoid shaving, as this tends to make the hair grow back thicker so regrowth will be visible sooner. A vicious circle. Ideally if you need to remove hair use tweezers for the odd one or wax instead.

Body Exfoliator

To make your own body exfoliator, or if you run out, there are loads of quick home recipes you can make yourself.

You can search online or at your library but basically mix equal parts of either sugar or salt with oil such as olive or coconut. For a gentle and quick alternative you can use just bicarbonate of soda.

The choice of oils, salts or sugars from your kitchen cupboards are endless; so have a play and use what suits you best.

Don't use on broken skin and the finer the grains the better, especially if you have sensitive skin, as a general rule.

If using left over bath salts to make an exfoliator, crush in a blender or pestle and mortar until fine, then add your oil a few drops at a time and mix. It is best to just mix a small amount at a time and use up to save storing in the fridge and avoiding any wastage.

Facial exfoliator

You can use bicarbonate of soda with a little water and then rinse too or add a bit to your cleanser a few drops of oil for a gentler version.

| **Hair removal** | As above avoid shaving. Below are some of the alternatives for you to think about. | |

Hair removal

As above avoid shaving. Below are some of the alternatives for you to think about.

Use less cream for removal or bleaching hair and avoid the temptation to apply to an even greater area of skin.

You could just pluck—little and often is the key. This will help cut down on the more aggressive and costly options. Good for very sensitive skin, which doesn't' get on with creams and shaving.

Waxing reduces regrowth so in the long run will reduce use.

Shaving for men

For wet shaving use a brush to apply the gel or cream. You can use less, as you lather up this way. Also if you need to shave an area again, you can just use the brush again which will have some lather still left in, before you rinse and store away to dry. (*A tip from my husband, 2013*).

Glass and tiles in the shower

To avoid having to clean so much and reduce your use of lime scale removers/vinegar, once you have finished using the shower use a screen wiper on your glass shower and tiles. This means the shower looks cleaner for longer as you have removed the water from the shower walls. This reduces any lime scale forming too from the drying water droplets on your surfaces. An absolute godsend and time saver when it comes to trying to reduce lime scale. Also, if you always do this, your shower will be cleaner for longer saving you time and effort. If you do not have a screen wiper use a dry cloth, or your towel once you're finished and then put in the wash.

I came across this idea in Germany years ago and it has made a huge difference ever since.

Mirrors

No need to buy any glass cleaner. Use a microfiber cloth, usually the drier the cloth the better the results. Microfibre cloths pick up the dirt without the aid of chemicals, so they're a total winner in terms of saving money, time and the environment.

(*EnviroProducts Ltd, 2013*)

Chrome

You do not need any chrome cleaners—just dry off with a microfibre cloth. If you want to remove lime scale, use vinegar with a normal cloth first.

Mould

To remove mould you can use Bicarbonate of soda (*Dr. Oetker, 2014*) You can also use vinegar, which is my favourite way.

(*blacktoxicmolds.com, 2014*)

Bathroom bin

For the toilet bin, use a bin liner. It saves time, smells and washing out. Don't buy special bin liners, re-use cereal packet plastic bags, a small chemist bag, or even old frozen pea bags. My favourite is a toilet roll plastic wrapper, just cut across the top to open up one end. Saves going downstairs to get another plastic bag too.

Recycling made easy

Have a pedal bin in the bathroom for all the non-recyclable stuff. For what you can recycle do not put in the bin but leave on the side. Take downstairs when you remember on your way down and put in the proper recycling container straight away. Saves time sorting later.

If you use toilet paper to blow your nose, that can go in the toilet too. Most plastic bottles can be recycled. So can most lids, the easy trick is if you can bend the lid enough to stick into a milk bottle for example then it is recyclable.

Glass cosmetic bottles can be recycled. Remove caps and lids. These lids are made of much harder plastic and have no give in them and are usually black in colour. They feel more like plastic around your landline phone as an example; and are not the same polymers of plastic as in food packaging and general household consumable packaging like shampoo or washing up liquid for instance. Should the packaging change in the future for the better, you will be able to know what can and can't be recycled in the household waste collection system.

All metal items can be recycled but for various reasons are likely to not get recycled if you put them out with your cans. So what you can do is have an old Quality Street tin or similar and fill with all sorts of bits of metal or mainly metal items, such as paper clips, razor blades, foil, metal chains, springs in lids, screw caps, jar lids etc. When full put the lid on and take to the recycling centre 'tip' and drop in the big metal skip for metal along with the big items i.e. broken bikes, camping chairs etc. A bit more of the extra mile with recycling, but why not? It all helps.

Laundry/utility room/ house maintenance

Principles

✓ Don't spin it, hang it!

✓ Use less chemicals

Horrendous Household fact:

'Washing machines vary tremendously in how much water they use per wash: when adjusted for capacity, some use as much as 20 litres per kilogram while others as little as 6 litres per kilogram! Therefore, when buying a new washing machine it is important to make sure that the model is water efficient.' (*Waterwise, 2013. P7*).

Fresh air is a wonderful free resource which is often forgotten about. It is the best way to air the house, dry clothes and debug rugs, with no need for any sprays or tumble dryers.

I cannot stress enough the benefits of using fewer chemical – apart from the money you'll save! The fewer chemicals you have the better, as they can pollute the air in your home. They can be an irritant and corrosive, so I suggest that before you spray them onto kitchen surfaces, in bathrooms where they come into direct contact with your skin or potentially on the food your family eat you read the label, check the contents list and health warnings. Chemicals can damage your possessions with spills and need to be locked away from young children, as they can be poisonous too. As you spend a lot of time breathing in the air in your home every day it is worth checking the contents of your sprays, especially if you have any allergies, eczema, or even more importantly asthma. This view seems to be shared by the (*American Lung Association, 2013*).

Below is a list of ways you can cut down on chemicals. The smaller the cocktail of chemicals in your home the less likely you are to develop allergies to them, and if you do develop an allergy, it can be easier to identify. My particular pet hate are sprays, as these tend to make whatever the aggressive chemical that you (not everyone) might be irritated by, airborne and more able to cause hay fever and eczema-like symptoms or in my case, with asthma-related breathing difficulties too.

Gadgets	Lots of gadgets we buy we then don't really use that much. Instead we leave them on standby and forget about them– in the garage, perhaps. Turn them off, hire instead of buy, or even better, sell them. Do we really need an electric carving knife when a proper carving knife will last a lifetime and will not need any energy? The same will be true for a lot of other items. So go ahead and de-clutter.	
Energy Efficiency	For ways of making your home more energy efficient go to the energy section for loads of tips. Also there are various grants, advice and support out there to make your home more energy efficient, and you will be surprised to find out how much could be free. See energy section for more details.	
Appliance maintenance	Make sure your appliances are working properly. Simple things to check out for: Check your oven door seal is not letting any heat escape – easy to spot as you can usually see the steam trail on the outside of the door. If you need to replace this, it is easy and inexpensive to do so. Make sure your fridge and freezer door seals are working properly and defrost regularly or when you notice the build-up of ice. Avoid putting the appliance next to a heat source such as a radiator or cooker or in direct sunlight. For more details see energy section. Regularly empty out your tumble dryer filter. The fluff can go on the compost heap.	
Water meter	If you don't have a water meter, this is something worth considering, as you will be paying for the amount you are using instead of a fixed rate for your property. Your water supplier should fit a water meter at no charge to you. Ideal if you do not waste water and there are only a few people living in your home. Contact your local water supplier for advice and installation. See link to OFWAT leaflet at back.	

Washing machines

Wash your clothes on a programme with a lower temperature setting, and make sure each wash load is full to reduce the amount of washing you do. Also use a short washing cycle as much as possible.

Modern washing powders and liquids now work just as well on lower temperatures. Washing clothes at 30 degrees instead of a higher temperature uses around 40% less energy. See link to (*Which, 2015*)

A full load in your washing machine uses half the water of two small loads. (*Thames Water, 2014*). Therefore if you have a pile of clothes that needs washing with some delicates where you can't use the spin cycle, to save doing two separate washes just don't use the spin cycle.

Spin your clothes in the washing machine on the highest spin cycle to remove as much water as possible. This means clothes will dry quicker so there will be less need for the tumble dryer.

Wash dark colours (socks, jeans, briefs, dark t-shirts, kitchen cloths, sponges) at 30°C. No spin is required.

Light colours: (work/school shirts, t-shirts, light underwear, towels, bedding). Depending on the mix wash at 30°C or 40°C with or without spin. You can rub a stain remover onto collars and cuffs and put them in at 30°C with the rest of the lights if you wish.

An energy-efficient washing machine will save money on your electricity bill and on your water bill if you have a meter. (*Energy Saving Trust, 2015*). If you are planning on buying a new washing machine, choosing an Energy Saving Trust recommended model will save you money on your energy bills and water bills with each and every wash over the lifetime of the appliance. Look out for the logo.

Ensure you get your old electrical items recycled. The easiest way is to get advice from the shop where you are buying the item. They also may provide an uplift and recycle service. Alternatively take to your local council Household Waste Recycling Site if not selling or freecycling. For more information on freecycling go to the Freecycle link at the back of the book.

DID YOU KNOW
'Your washing machine alone accounts for 7% of your energy bill' (uswitch, 2015)

Detergent

Use eco-friendly washing power, it is kinder to your clothes so they keep their shape and colour longer. To save energy, check the packaging on your detergent as you may be able to wash at a colder temperature than you thought. This goes for all your cleaners; the new and improved detergents of today might not always need such high water temperatures.

Another alternative to standard detergent is to use washing soda or soda crystals, they are cheaper and do the job just as well. Follow instructions on pack and don't put directly onto clothes; use the soap dispenser drawer. Great for keeping colours too.

Eco-balls are another alternative to standard detergent. Just pop the 2 Eco-balls on top of your washing load at the back (ideally not quite full so they can do their thing) and you can use them for an amazing 240 washes! Did you know Eco-balls are antibacterial and they raise the alkalinity of the water to above pH10? Bacteria are active between pH6 and pH8. (*Ecozone, 2014*) You can also refill them when you need to. Needless to say this is a huge saving compared to detergent and softener if you still use it. Ideal for coloureds. More on fabric softener below.

You can also get Soap Nuts, which use nature's soft and natural cleansing power to get your clothes clean and smelling fresh. These are cheaper than using detergents and allergy free, so they're a must to try. See link at the back of the book for supplier. (*Salveo, 2013*). I find these are much better at keeping colours bright and prevent fading compared to mainstream supermarket detergents.

Whatever detergent you use – natural or otherwise – it is always best to treat stains before you put clothes in the wash; there are some ideas below in the stains section.

Your whites

If your whites aren't as white as you'd like, try the sun. Hang them on the washing line, on an airier inside the house or lie them flat on a towel for a more natural way of drying.

My favourite alternative to reaching for the strong stuff is to wash with some Eco-laundry bleach when you want to occasionally use something stronger to keep whites white. The good news is they do not contain bleach or optical brighteners. I use Ecover laundry bleach, still green and kind; it does the trick for me. See link at the back for further details.

Brighten colours in wash

You can use soda crystals or washing soda in your wash to brighten colours. I prefer Soap Nuts or Eco-balls which work just as well if not better on their own. *In fact, compared to normal detergents these three alternatives are far superior in my opinion.*

Stains

Bicarbonate of soda

An alternative to bleach in general is sodium bicarbonate/ bicarbonate of soda. Sprinkle on damped stains including wine, grease, grimy shirt collars, dirt and mould. You can also add a bit of distilled white vinegar and mix together if you wish. I prefer to use slightly cooled boiled water if suitable for carpets or fabrics.

Fizzy water

If you have any stains on carpets for example try a little clear soda or fizzy clear water instead of tap water first to help lift out the stain. This may save you using any other cleaner. (eHow, 2013)

Salt

I once dropped half a bottle of red wine on a cream woollen Persian carpet and at the time didn't use bicarbonate of soda. I dried it with a towel to soak up as much wine as possible, tipped some white wine on it (which was a waste of time, drink it instead is my advice.) Then I used washing up liquid and a brush and in the end I tentatively used salt with a little hot water and rubbed it in and left it for the night as it was working. I vacuumed up the salt and reapplied. I still have

(continued over)

Boiling water

this beautiful rug – without a stain. Wonderful! I now use salt on red wine stains on linen before they go in the wash at 40°C. Brilliant and saves using a hotter wash.

A drop or two of boiling water can sometimes be all you need to get out a stubborn food stain.

Soda crystals are also good cleaning product for wine, tea and coffee stains. (*Mistral Lab Supplies, 2014*)

I give this final suggestion because it is better than throwing something away.

If all else fails, at your own risk on linen whites only, here's a little tip that might remove the stain. Adding a little drop of diluted bleach indoors on an impossible stain can do the trick, but you will have to watch over it and remove as it will lift before your eyes within seconds if not a couple of minutes and needs to be rinsed out straight away. If left on, it will remove all colours from the cloth and it will go yellow, which can never be fixed, so be warned! I give this tip because I believe it is better to use a little bleach than throwing something away because the stain appears permanent.

Blood stains

Rinse in **COLD** water with soap, then add into your normal wash as usual. It's OK to let item dry if you aren't putting them in the washing machine straight away.

Soaking

Save up a few items and soak together depending on colours. It could reduce hand washing needed. Use soda crystals if grimy.

Reduce your dry cleaning bill

Reduce your dry cleaning bill by avoiding buying dry clean only items and/or just use a stain remover if that is all that is needed—and of course remember to air your clothes. If your washing machine has a delicates setting you may be able to use this. Once you have enough clothes you can add them to make a full load. Or try hand washing them in lukewarm water with a mild detergent and straighten and/or dry flat. Ideal for jumpers. Check the label for the manufactures recommendations and be guided by them to avoid ruining your garment.

Shower curtains

Wash with bicarbonate of soda to get rid of stains and mould. Do this by hand or add to your washing machine when washing towels with your normal detergent for whites. For best results allow to drip dry back on the shower curtain rail.

(*Readers Digest, 2013*).

Fabric softener

You don't need to use fabric softer for every wash, just dry clothes on your washing line as normal without it. Ideal for darks wash such as socks, underwear and various synthetic fibres, jeans etc.

If you have a tumble dryer you can use eco-balls that bounce around in the drum and will give you the fluffiest towels without even a teaspoon of fabric softener! You can use these again and again so they are a real bargain compared to fabric softener and are cheap to buy at under £10 a pair. They also reduce drying time by 25% (*dryerballs Ltd, 2012*) and therefore save you 25% on your energy consumption to dry those clothes!

I absolutely love these balls!!

If you have micro-fibre towels or cloths you shouldn't use any fabric softener, as they need to be free from any products that coat the fabric.

To remove any product residue soak for a short while in boiling water or rewash. (*EnviroProducts Ltd, 2013*)

Airing clothes

You don't always need to wash everything after wearing once if you haven't stained the garment, maybe it needs just airing. You can air inside on a hanger in the room (not in the wardrobe) or over the back of chair or outside on the washing line. If it does not smell fresh after two days always put it in the washing basket. When you wash your clothes over time the colours can fade and they lose shape, so you are saving money in clothes buying in the long run too by not washing them unnecessarily.

Don't spin

Hang your clothes to dry on the line outside and/or use a clotheshorse inside. Some shirts can be dried straight on a hanger. This will save on ironing. It's best to have an airier hanging from the ceiling or wall over the bath or in a utility room. It's quick, easy and convenient. Or you might have an airing cupboard you can use.

Let the heat out

Drying clothes directly on the radiators should be avoided. Your boiler will need to work harder than it needs to (*British Gas, 2013*). Put a clotheshorse near to the radiator instead. This will help dry clothes and let the radiator heat the room at the same time.

Tumble dryer or no tumble dryer solutions

Microfibre towels are amazing!

If you have a tumble dryer, get yourself some eco-balls as mentioned above, which you place in the drum. They cut down your drying time (*British Gas, 2013*) and therefore save you energy.

In my experience, towels and dressing gowns are the only things that need to go in the tumble dryer to get them really fluffy. If you don't have a tumble dryer switch to microfibre towels; they are super-soft and they don't need or want. They come out as new, fluffy, every time. They also dry really quickly, unlike normal towels so they're great when time and space are important too.

Make sure you don't tumble dry needlessly. Set your dryer

Tumble dryer or no tumble dryer solutions

(continued)

to a short drying time, and if need be put it on again for a short period. Once almost dry you can remove clothes and line dry them. Towels will still be fluffy and this will save energy. Everything else can be line dried or flat dried. If you need something more quickly then you will need the dryer but remove sooner than later to avoid wasting energy.

If you don't have a tumble dryer or outdoor place to dry clothes, make sure your washing machine is set to use its maximum spin cycle, to help dry your wash quickly by removing as much water as possible. If you don't have a garden or utility room or the space in the bathroom to hang clothes you may need to use the tumble dryer more often. Make sure you maintain your equipment by cleaning out the filter regularly. (*British Gas, 2013*) The fluff from the filter can go on the compost heap.

If you can't do without a tumble dryer but don't really need to use it a lot, you could opt for a combined washer/dryer, which usually dries half the load. This is a great space saving idea saving you money compared to buying two separate machines. There are various varies and options available so check the small print before you buy.

Ironing

A personal favourite of mine, not.

Avoid ironing where possible and/or cut down ironing time. Hang garments outside or indoors on an airier to reduce ironing, or you can use coat hangers if you wish too. Dry other clothes like jumpers flat on a clean bath towel outside or inside. You can keep a spare 'past its best' towel for this with your laundry products if you like.

Ironing shirts

To iron cotton shirts, dry on a hanger, and ideally iron when still slightly damp, that way there's no need for the mist spray. The same goes for all your linen. If the shirt is too dry use a mist sprayer filled with tap water. No need for any special sprays. If you have no sprayer, use a cup of tap water, dip your hands in and flick a little water onto the garment.

If iron your bedding, use the above suggestions too. But this too can be avoided by buying microfibre bedding.

| **Odours** | Bicarbonate of soda is also great at absorbing odours from smelly shoes, damp clothes that need washing again to pet smells. Just leave the jar with the lid off in the room or sprinkle some on the item. (The Soap Kitchen, 2014)

Vinegar also absorbs odours in the room, so if you wish, leave a jar of vinegar with the lid off in the room instead of using your conventional air freshener. Also great for eliminating smoke odours. (*Environix, 2014*) | |

| **Go bananas** | Go bananas and use a banana skin to clean your leather items. Rub the inside of the skin on the shoe and then polish to a shine with a cloth or brush in the usual way. (*Readers Digest, 2013*)

For a wonderful shiny finish, use old socks as cloths to polish shoes and silver after using a banana skin.

You can also use a different old sock to apply your normal polish.

Banana skins or bananas you can't eat can also be used to polish wood. Rub onto the wood and then polish with a dry cloth – ideally a microfibre one. What works for shoes I find works for wood too. | |

| **Cut down on chemicals** | The smaller the range of products you buy to clean your house, the better. Less carrying, storage, clutter, allergies and of course cost, not to mention reduced pollution. | |

| **Dilute cleaners** | Even the non-concentrated ones are usually stronger than they need to be, so add water and mix to make them last longer. Ideal for washing up liquid. | |

Washing up

Only squirt what you need. If you are finding you have cleaning potential left after you have done the washing up, use less next time and use the rest now to clean worktops, kitchen cupboards, ornaments etc. until all suds are used up.

Alternatively, as above, add tap water to the washing up liquid bottle and give it a quick shake. Next time when you squirt you will be using less liquid, making your washing liquid go further.

Keep an old washing up liquid bottle if you like and add up to a 1/3 of water to your washing liquid or keep topping up your liquid bottle with water until you are happy you have the right strength for your washing up bowl.

Buy concentrated products

Concentrated products are usually better value for money, and you can add the water yourself as above. Just remember to check the packaging and use less of it otherwise you have saved nothing. It is even easier to squirt too much! Remember if something lasts so much longer then you need to squirt so much less!

Use kinder alternatives

Using eco-detergents is kinder to the environment and also kinder to your skin. You can save in not so obvious ways, too, by using an eco-friendly washing-up liquid for example, which is kinder to hands and so will save you money on the amount of creams you use to moisturize cracked, itchy skin.

Using too much or non-eco washing powders or cleaning products is more likely to aggravate sensitive skin and/or lungs. The less detergents you use the better. *BUPA UK (2013)*, Asthma *UK (2013)*. Signs of overuse or reactions include itchy, dry, flaky skin or lots of little bumps like a rash on the skin, rubbing eyes or a combination of all of these ailments, as well as breathing problems such as asthma. If it says it's an irritant on the back of the bottle – beware!

To cut through grease

My favourite is vinegar!

Use vinegar or lemon juice (including the bottled variety) or to cut through grease. It is a greener, cheaper and safer alternative to aggressive chemicals that are usually an irritant in some measure. Squirt on surface area, rub in and rinse off with clean water.

After a roast dinner, use any left over hot water in pots or the kettle to rinse all pots and roasting trays with a quick once round with the brush. This makes life a lot easier.

If that does not do the trick, add some vinegar straight away while the pan is still hot or heat some vinegar in the pan for a minute and then scrub if needed instead of grabbing for the chemicals. *(Allergy UK, 2013)*

Soda crystals are a very good way to cut through greasy surfaces. The same goes for Bicarbonate of soda.

Lime scale

Vinegar does the trick. Leave on for a few minutes if needed. Great for descaling kettles too. *(Allergy UK, 2013)*

You can use leftover vinegar as well as new, when the pickle jar has been emptied of onions, gherkins or whatever; put it under the sink with the cleaning products and use as needed for cleaning.

Cleaning certain metals

Cleaning brass, copper and silver is not something we do every day, so before buying a specific cleaner sitting idle in the cupboard most of the year here are a few alternatives.

Firstly most metals are nowadays coated with a varnish to stop them tarnishing, so the first thing to remember is not to remove the protective varnish layer. Therefore first of all just use a dry soft cloth or a microfibre cloth and rub to see if the tarnish comes off. A little bicarbonate of soda might be all you need.

For copper pots, back to my favourite cleaner, vinegar. Use a

Cleaning certain metals *(continued)*	sauce with a lot of vinegar in it, such as ketchup, or immerse in plain vinegar for a while depending on discolouration, then wipe away. You can also add salt and rub with a cloth if you wish, but the vinegar is the show stopper. *(Homeguides, 2013)*	
Marks and stains	Try bicarbonate of soda, soda crystals, salt and/or vinegar first before using a branded cleaner. These natural cleaning products are cheaper and more versatile and in my opinion better at cleaning all manner of things. Cutting down on the range of specific cleaners saves storage space too.	
Mould	To remove mould you can use Bicarbonate of soda *(Dr. Oetker, 2014)* You can also use vinegar, which is my favourite way. *(blacktoxicmolds.com, 2014)*	
Cleaning windows	Avoid all sprays. The traditional approach to polishing is to wash with water then wipe with diluted vinegar and polish with newspaper. I prefer the modern day alternative. Just use a microfibre cloth. Add no chemicals and with very little or no water wipe the glass or mirror until it is smear free. If glass is dirty you can wash with soapy water or wipe the odd spot with a little vinegar and a cloth, rinse and finish off with the microfibre cloth so you have no residue or smears.	

Net curtains	Hand or machine wash on a delicates setting with bicarbonate of soda on a wash cycle with no spin. Drip dry in position to avoid creases and do not iron.	

Cleaning floors	With carpets being out of fashion and wood, stone or laminate flooring being in, this means you do not need to use the vacuum cleaner as much. Use a broom, ideally a microfibre broom and/or a mop instead.	

Dusting	No need to use any sprays. Instead use a microfibre cloth and a small amount of water. This picks up the dust instead of just moving it around. Rinse out and dry when finished to use another day. Occasionally wash in washing machine with colours (remember without fabric softener) or let soak in some left over boiling water in a bowl. To reduce dust, have a natural fibre door mat and remember to take your shoes off in the house.	

Furniture polish	On occasion you will want to polish rather than just dust your wooden furniture. For wood use a tiny amount of olive oil on a soft clean cloth to polish. A little goes a long way. Amazing. Removes all those sticky marks too. (*Readers Digest, 2013*) You can also use banana. I prefer to use the skin as it's quicker, easier and less messy – and you can just save the skin after eating your banana! A little more elbow grease is needed than with the olive oil. You can't eat the skin of a banana, so you might as well put it to some other use!	

Ants

Instead of buying chemicals to get rid of them, pour boiling water along their trail, especially before they enter the house. Keep sugar and other sugary things in an airtight tub or tin as well, to stop them coming back. You can use an old ice cream tub if you wish.

Draft excluder

For the back door or other doors leading to the outside make sure there is no draught at the bottom of the door. If there is, buy draft excluders to keep the heat in. If you don't want to buy a draught excluder, you can make a long snake or sausage dog the length of the bottom of the door and fill with all sorts of left over material for a homely and free alternative.

Repair

If you have household or garden items in need of repair visit a spare parts website or go to the manufacturer's website to buy the relevant spare part you need. Espares.co.uk sells spare parts for most electrical items - and features free, easy-to-understand videos on how to repair common household items. There are lots of video guides to choose from – such as 'how to replace a spray arm on your dishwasher'.

Reusing

If old t-shirts, towels or socks etc. are not 'good enough' for the charity shop, reuse them as cleaning clothes and cut up as necessary. Keep the torn towel to dry the dog or keep to one side to dry your jumpers.

Save your old toothbrushes, they are ideal for cleaning in hard to reach areas.

Mend

Repair clothes and soft furnishings before thinking of replacing them. Likewise with shoes and boots – get them mended.

Old tools

Donate your old tools you don't need any more to local charities directly or to your local charity shop. Alternatively go to your local car boot and make yourself a little bit of money too. A great way to spring clean and de-clutter.

Recycling made easy

All metal is recyclable, so have a metal tin – such as an old metal sweet tin—where you put all odd small metal bits. When full and you are passing by, drop off at the recycling centre or 'tip'.

Rubbish collection

There's no need to buy bin liners. Use the old spare plastic bags you have around the house to line your pedal bin and then put them in your wheelie bin. There is no need to line the wheelie bin with a black plastic bag.

If you do not have a wheeled bin and your council requires you to have a black bag for household waste collection, try to minimise your general waste by recycling as much as you can to avoid the need for so many black plastic bags.

Hazardous household waste

Old paint and varnish tins are hazardous waste, so treat them carefully, along with paint thinners and brush cleaners. Also a few everyday items are also hazardous waste, which include: descaler, stain remover, oven cleaners, drain cleaners, glues and batteries. Don't forget the more unusual waste items such as electrical equipment, gas cylinders and equipment containing cathode ray tubes (e.g. televisions, computer monitors). None of these should be disposed of in your waste bin. Take them instead to the local 'tip' or household waste recycling site. For advice and a full list of items, visit your local council website.

Used Batteries

Even though these are hazardous waste you can recycle them at certain supermarkets other outlets or even at work, so you can save on a trip to the recycling centre. Alternatively save up and take them to your nearest battery recycling point.

Bedroom

Principles

✓ Create a calm and unpolluted environment

Horrendous Household fact:

'It has been estimated that every home in the UK could reduce the amount of energy it uses by 20%.' (Act on Energy, 2013).

Heaven for me is a clutter free life, especially in the bedroom. Seeing stuff all around where it does not belong does not make for a relaxing environment and just reminds me of extra work that needs doing. It also creates extra effort in terms of finding what you're looking for. I am sure you will agree. Why move stuff from A to B and clean around instead of putting it where it belongs?

Below are some helpful hints that you can use in the bedroom and perhaps other rooms in the house too.

Too hot under the covers	Usually when we put the heating on it is because it is too cold downstairs in the lounge. Why then is the heating on in the bedrooms for half the night? If needed you could set these radiators at a much cooler setting and/or turn these up an hour before the heating goes off for the night.	

Light touch	Remember to turn off the lights when not in the room – see more tips for lights in the energy section to help with this.	

Freshen rooms	Freshen rooms by airing, not spraying. Air the house ideally in the middle of the day when the outside temperature is at its highest, while the heating is off in winter to reduce heat loss from the house. If you are not in the house during lunchtime, do it as soon as possible in the afternoon.	

Air freshener	Instead of buying air fresheners use up that old perfume if you can't open the window.	

The easiest way to freshen a room is to leave a small jar of vinegar in the room, or a tablespoon of bicarbonate of soda on a dish. The great thing about these two methods is that you can reuse the vinegar and bicarbonate of soda afterwards as normal to clean with. Both vinegar and bicarbonate of soda absorb odours. (*Dri-Pak Ltd, 2014*), (*Environix, 2014*)

You can make your own air freshener if you wish at a fraction of the price by diluting vinegar, which is a powerful deodorizer, with up to equal parts water. Great at removing smoke and food odours from your home. Ehow.com list a few recipes you could use too such as using citrus and vanilla as well. Ideal if you have some spare. Alternatively just leave the citrus peel on a dish for a while when you use some fruit before putting on the compost heap or in the food recycling bin.

Smelly feet/ shoes	Put a teaspoon of bicarbonate of soda in your shoe and tap a few times so it covers the inside of the shoe and leave in. Wear as usual. Dust over the soles of your feet. Bicarbonate of soda absorbs odours (*Dri-Pak Ltd, 2014*) No need to buy a foot spray.	

Damp dusting	Avoid buying or using sprays. Use water to wet a cloth and wring out, then damp dust surfaces. If dusting wood furniture use a soft cloth with a tiny amount of water and follow with a wipe of a dry cloth. Best of all use a microfibre cloth. Damp dusting is more effective and lasts much longer than using a dry conventional duster as it picks up the dust. Better for those people with dust allergies too. *(Asthma UK, 2013)*	

Mirrors	Avoid buying chemical products. Wet a leather cloth, wring out and wipe. If greasy use a little vinegar on another cloth first. For windows you could use newspaper and vinegar, followed by a rubber wiper and cloth to finish. *I use a microfibre nowadays.* The quickest, modern way is to use a microfibre cloth. This is also a good option, especially for the odd finger mark. Just use with almost no water to wipe the surface for best results. Remember: no chemicals on the microfibre cloth of any kind and no fabric softener. If you put chemicals on a microfibre cloth by mistake you need to wash out the chemicals. You can do this by soaking the cloth in some left over boiled kettle water and then rinsing and wringing out.	

Mattresses	You can sprinkle Bicarbonate of soda on your mattress to remove stains. Leave on for the day or as long as possible and then vacuum off. Or make a thick paste with water leave to dry and vacuum off. *(Dr. Oetker, 2014)*	

Bedding	After washing leave your bedding outside to dry. Sunlight works well on your bedding as it can kill bed mites. *(NHS, 2014)*	

Tidy up

Less cutter means less housework, which saves time as well as improving your living environment. If you don't need it or like it, take it to the charity shop or sell it. Once something has been tidied up you will feel in a much more positive mood, as well as having found some money, that odd sock or earing you've been looking for, or that piece of the puzzle that has been missing for a long time.

If you do not have enough storage space, have a clear-out or buy a cupboard or wardrobe so everything can be put away easily without creating an eyesore or a nuisance.

This might be the time to admit you have too many clothes and donate to the charity shop.

Cupboards and the like

Large furniture, especially wardrobes, provides a good layer of insulation, so put them against an outside wall of the house. Also keep them away from the windows so they do not block any light, ideally put them in the darkest part of the room.

Curtains

You can get second hand ones at charity shops or online at specialist second hand curtain shops such as The Curtain Exchange, see details at the back.

Mend or move on

If clothes need repairing, mend them. If they don't fit, alter them yourself or get someone else to do it for you. You could give them to a friend or relative if that is appropriate or alternatively donate them to a charity shop, or sell.

Some shops trade in second hand clothes. They give you a percentage of the sale price, once sold. You can even find some vintage designer second hand shops now where you can buy or sell some amazing stuff.

Swishing

Swapping clothes – or Swishing, as it is now known – is also coming into fashion, with various events and clothes swapping websites. See details at the back of the book.

You can buy second hand at Asos Marketplace. See link at back of book. Some stores might take old clothes back and give you money off vouchers, so keep an eye out for these deals such as Marks and Spencer, which currently have an arrangement with Oxfam. See link at back of book.

Making your own clothes

Making your own clothes, repairing and altering them, is a wonderful hobby to have and a must if you have some high vintage clothes that need a little alteration or repair.

When making from scratch you could spend a lot of money making a dress that you could buy cheaper in a shop, so there are a few things to consider if not using that gorgeous fabric for a special occasion. If you do not have a sewing machine, borrow one or go on a course before you buy. Reconditioned sewing machines are cheaper or of course you can buy second hand, and the web will be the easiest way of finding what you are looking for. Use second hand shops or go online for materials, including patterns. The same goes for knitting needles and wool.

The greatest savings are in altering and mending clothes, and this is a great way to ensure you always have a fresh and unique look; so have a go.

Borrow sewing books from the library or buy from a second hand shop. If you have a bit of experience you soon realise you don't always need a pattern; you can copy from something you already have that fits.

Look after your things

If you look after your clothes and shoes they will look better and last a lot longer. Use shoetrees or stuff the fronts of shoes with tissue paper and stack the shoes in their boxes. You can use old newspaper too if you don't have spare tissue but beware that newsprint can rub off and onto your hands

Look after your things
(continued)

as well, so only use for black shoes and check your hands are clean before picking up the cream shoes or any clothes.

Keep the plastic wrapping from dry cleaned clothes and cover the more sensitive clothes or those you don't wear that often first, then the rest.

You can also turn your clothes inside out on the hanger to avoid dust and sunlight marking your clothes if storing in the wardrobe for a long time between wearing.

Air your clothes

If you air your clothes you will not need to wash them so often, and they will not wear out or lose their shape so quickly and the colour will stay bright longer. Ideal for jumpers in particular.

Downgrade clothes

No need for Prada while poop scooping!

Keep your best clothes for best.

Over time this will change for various reasons. At that point downgrade before giving to charity and wear them in the house when not going out. Then you have clothes you wear doing the housework, cleaning the car and/or gardening.

Finally save a really old pair of jeans with holes in and an old t-shirt for painting and decorating. This will save you money as it is all too easy to get a bit of bleach, paint or varnish on your clothes and then they are ruined for going out or even for around the house. So if there is a chance that you might get grass stains, or snag or tear your clothes change into your 'scruffs'.

Stockings or tights

Stockings, hold-ups or pop socks last longer than tights when you buy two matching pairs at a time. When you ladder one leg you have a spare leg, which you can use again. Buy the same variety again and keep going.

Use clear nail varnish to stop a ladder and you may get more wear out of it. Ideal if you want to wear tights under trousers when at home.

Those darn socks

A must for the young teenage girls who want to wear tights to school but keep making holes.

Repair socks before giving up on them. Darn or sew by hand or with a sewing machine. For thick tights and opaque tights it is a really quick and effective way to sew up the hole with a sewing machine, turning the socks or tights inside out first.

Bedtime tales

You can keep the bedrooms upstairs at a lower temperature than the living room downstairs. To keep more comfortable in bed on a cold night, use thicker bed covers in winter compared to summer.

Keep socks on in bed. If this is not sexy enough for you try some cute pink or blue fluffy ones that match your dressing gown to feel special. Or perhaps you prefer lace ones. These tend to roll down on a night, but usually you are fast asleep by then.

The pink fluffy ones are my favourite!

If you have an airing cupboard you can put your bedclothes in there so when you get to bed you have lovely warm clothes to put straight on.

Of course a hot water bottle is an old favourite and much better than putting on an electric blanket. The current new thing in hot water bottles are waterless microwaveable ones in the shape of teddy bears.

Do all these things instead of turning the heating up in the bedrooms and you will save energy and have reduced heating bills.

Keep chemicals out

Chemicals should be in the utility room, kitchen or bathroom and not anywhere else. Move toiletries, cologne and nail varnish into the bathroom to aid a better night's sleep.

For those with allergies like me this is worth bearing in mind. The less allergic reactions you have to stuff, the less medicines and potions and lotions you need to buy to fix them.

Soft toys

If you want to debug your soft toys, a good way is to vacuum them, put them in a plastic bag and then in the freezer for a few days. Thereafter vacuum again and if necessary hand wash. A good time to mend any tears so it will look as good as new. This helps with the life of the teddy and means you will not feel the urge to buy a new one if you think the old one is too unhealthy for your young child to cuddle or teeth on.

You can also wash the teddy in the washing machine with your darks and then line dry if you wish.

My daughter's little red hippo still looked cute with one ear attached to the washing line on a summer's day!

All of the above work well for your pet's soft toys too.

Spare bedroom

Turn the heating off and keep the door closed most of the time for the rooms in the house which are not being used. Air occasionally when the heating in the house is off. Keep curtains open. Ensure the door fits well or add insulation tape around the door.

Recycling made easy

For bedrooms – especially children's rooms – use two bins, one for paper and one for general waste. If you don't have a spare bin you can use an old sturdy paper bag that you get given from some shops when you buy clothes for example. Take bottles and cans and apple cores downstairs. This is easy to sort out if the kids put them in the non-paper bin. Line all bins with old plastic bags for clean and easy handling (except the paper bin). No need to wash out bins this way.

Chill Out Room Dining room/Lounge

Principles

✓ Create a cosy environment

Horrendous Household fact:

'Over £6M electrical items are thrown away each year in the UK and it's estimated that over half are still working or could easily be repaired.' (John Lewis Department Stores, 2013).

During our waking hours we all spend a lot of time in these rooms, especially the lounge, so we want it as cosy and comfortable as possible. So below are some handy hints to make your Chill Out room environmentally friendly and cost effective too. Not forgetting less housework – it is after all somewhere to chill out.

This zone is also where we all like to DIY so I have added some ideas and things to think about that could save pounds and the planet too.

TV/DVD/PS3	A TV, DVD player and PS3 will still use electricity when on standby, so switch them off. This could save you around £32 a year *(E.On, 2013)*.

Make sure the brightness setting on your TV is suitable for your room. The brighter the TV is set, the more energy it uses. The factory settings on TVs can often be too bright for home use so there is the potential here to save on your energy bill with very little effort and nothing more.

Encourage all your family to turn off equipment at the socket by making it easy to get to the switch, especially if away for the whole day let alone on holiday. Think about "losing" the remote control to the television to reduce the temptation to leave it on standby.

Consider investing in a smart energy-saving mains extension lead so that all the equipment linked to your TV (video recorder, DVD player, games controllers etc.) is automatically switched off whenever the TV is turned off.

If you don't want to buy new, clear a space around your plug sockets to make it easier to turn items off at the mains, and have the DVD recorder plug on a different switch so you can keep the power on if you need to record something.

At home, some people like a little background noise. If so, put the radio on instead of the TV. As a general rule the smaller the item the less power it uses *(Energy Saving Trust, 2014)*. Large flat screen TVs use a lot of energy in comparison.

Remember that the energy consumption of your TV is strongly linked to the screen-size. Smaller TVs will therefore generally be cheaper to run. If you are thinking about buying a new TV think carefully about how big a screen you actually need.

Keep doors closed	To help keep the warmth where you want it, keep doors closed for the rooms you are not using currently – e.g. the lounge during the day.

Keep the front and back doors closed. Close all doors when you go to bed at night. This is a good way of checking the radiators in a room are correctly set. When you walk in the

Keep doors closed
(continued)

room in the morning to open the curtains you can tell if the heating in that room is too high or low. This gives you the opportunity to fine-tune the radiators and keep the heat where you want it.

Doors and windows

Check you have no drafts and if you do, seal them up – including your letterbox. You might want to add a heavy curtain or rug over the front door. All this saves on heat loss and keeps the heat where you want it – in the rooms and not the hall and landing or worse, outside. For more details on insulating your home see the energy section.

If you are away at work all day do not be tempted to close the curtains hoping to stop the heat escaping. You are losing more by stopping the sunlight coming in and also not helping any potential damp problems, which will make you feel even colder.

Let the light in

Make sure curtains are fully open and if you are putting up new ones make sure the track runs beyond the window opening on both sides so curtains, when open, do not cover any of the window. This way the maximum amount of light can come into the room, helping to reduce the need for lights and heating. It also makes the room look much bigger and brighter.

Central heating system

Turn your thermostat down. Reducing your room temperature by 1°C could cut your heating bills by up to 10 per cent, a view shared by the (*Affordable Warmth Network, 2013, p17*). If you have a timer, set your heating and hot water to come on only when required rather than all the time. For more details on heating and hot water see energy section.

Radiators

Do not obstruct radiators with heavy furniture like sofas. The sofa gets nice and warm at the expense of the rest of the room. If that is the only place you can put the sofa, pull it away from the radiator as much as possible.

Radiator reflector panels

Radiator reflector panels can be fitted behind radiators to reflect the heat back into the room rather than heating the outside wall. This will aid convection—ideal for walls with no cavities i.e. solid brick walls or ones where there is no cavity wall insulation, but still a benefit whichever type of radiator you have with or without an insulated wall.

You could potentially save up to 20% on your heating bills with radiator reflectors. *(Joulesave, 2014)*

Radiator shelves

If you wish to fit a shelf, over the radiator is a good place. Just don't use MDF.

As hot air rises, the shelf helps push the heat from the radiator into the centre of the room. You will be able to turn the radiators down a little and still keep the same temperature in the centre of the room.

Decorating

Use light colours if decorating the walls as this will help keep the room brighter for longer in the day and therefore reduce the need for artificial light. Finish off old paint before buying new or donate to charity. If buying new, try the low VOC (Volatile Organic Compounds) paint.

DID YOU KNOW

'Lighting accounts for 7% of a typical household's energy bill.' *(Energy Saving Trust, 2013)*

Lights

Turn lights off in the room when you are not using them. Replace bulbs with low energy light bulbs. Ensure your bulb has the energy saving trust logo on it. Save the old ones to put back when leaving if you are renting or in case you run

Lights
(continued)

out. In other words don't just bin them. 'Dimming an old fashioned filament light usually saves energy.' (*Affordable Warmth Network, 2013, p13*).

Light bulbs come in a variety of options and the main energy saving light bulbs are Compact Fluorescent Lamps (CFLs) and Light Emitting Diodes (LEDs). Check the product information. Watts (w) measure power consumption

not brightness so to ensure you are getting the correct replacement bulb, check the lumen (lm) output too. The lifetime of the bulb is measured in hours (h). Also the light colour needs to be considered which is measured in Kelvins (K). For general light in the home 'soft white' or 'warm white' (2700-3200K) can be used. For use to work with or read by, choose 'cool white' (3200-4000K) or 'pure white' for clear vision with maximum colour rendering (100 Ra) is ideal for artists. For more details, the Energy Saving Trust provides useful information, as does Premium Light. See links at the back.

CFLs use 75-80% less electricity and can last up to ten times longer. A CFL lightbulb of the same brightness will save around £3 per year. (*Energy Saving Trust, 2013*)

LEDs are currently the most energy efficient lights with A+ ratings, (*Premium Light, 2014*). LEDs are particularly good for replacing spotlights and dimmable lights, and are fully bright almost straight away. (*Affordable Warmth Network, 2013, p12*). Replacing a halogen down-lighter with an LED alternative you could save around £40 per year on your electricity bill. They are more expensive to buy, but you will save in the long term. (*Energy Saving Trust, 2013*)

If all of this above is a bit too much to remember, a good rule of thumb when replacing old bulbs with CFL or LEDs is to replace an old 100w bulb with a new energy efficient 20w bulb. CFLs use roughly 20% of the energy and LEDs use 10% less than.

Modern strip lights with good reflector mountings are an efficient option, ideal for kitchens or above bathroom mirrors where bright light is required (*Energy Saving Trust, 2014*).

Lights (continued) 	Shades on lamps can darken the room; so choose carefully when buying new. Think about what sort of light you need and where it should be in the room. Having a range of lights in a room, all with separate switches, will make it easier to achieve the lighting you want and need, whenever and wherever you want it.	
Timed light switches	Timed light switches might be a good option. They turn off in a couple of minutes if using a pressure switch. These are ideal for the hall/landing and are cheap and easy to install. Motion sensor lights detect motion so come on and then turn off after a minute if they sense no movement. Either option is ideal for the hall. You could also investigate where else in the house you could fit these sensors. There are various on the market and prices start from around £15 each.	
Carpets or not?	Carpets require more cleaning and care than wooden, stone or laminate flooring. That means more vacuuming and cleaning products for stains, which costs in energy bills and shopping for chemicals or vacuum cleaner bags. If you have pets or allergies the less carpet the better. Have the odd nice rug instead which you can beat and leave outside in the sunlight for a bit if you wish – say an hour to help kill dust mites. (NHS, 2014)	
Wooden Skirting boards and fixtures	For wooden doorframes, doors, skirting boards, windowsills, varnish instead of painting. It is easier to keep them clean and involves less maintenance, and no repainting is needed to freshen up. Saves on DIY costs.	

Sustainable timber labelling

If buying timber or furniture look for FSC® label to ensure you are buying the best product.

The Forest Stewardship Council® (FSC) label is used on products ranging from floorboards and furniture to birthday cards and toilet paper. It shows that the wood used in a product has come from a forest that:

- Is well managed and follows strict FSC standards, from protecting the rights of people who live there to cutting down trees in a sustainable way.

- Has been independently inspected.

For further reading go to Forest Stewardship Council website, details at the back.

Window sills

Less maintenance is required on windowsills if they are either varnished wood or stone and not painted. Painted windowsills require more cleaning and maintenance. They also look tired really quickly.

Windows

Double glazed windows are very good at keeping the heat in the house.

If you wish to buy them, you need to be aware it is likely to be a long time before you recoup the money you've spent in energy bill savings, but double-glazing might add value to your house price. Seek advice before you spend.

If you need to buy new windows or replace glass go for A+ Rated energy efficiency ones. *See more details in the energy section.*

Curtains

Lined or thicker curtains will add another layer to keep the heat in at night and cut out draughts. Or you could add a thick thermal liner to the back of your old curtains or hang this layer separately between the window and your existing curtains. (*Energy Saving Trust, 2014*)

A good rule is to draw curtains at dusk.

An enclosed wooden pelmet or a curtain track that is flush ensures that no light gets in or out and also helps to reduces heat loss and cut down on draughts.

Rugs

If you have rugs, occasionally take them outside instead of vacuuming.

To kill some of the bugs, hang the rug over the washing line and use a beater or broom to remove the dust, or pick up two corners and beat the rug against an outside wall then put it out in sunlight for a short while. This way loads of dust and stuff comes out and the sunlight helps to kill bugs like house dust mites.

This can also reduce your vacuuming needs.

What lies beneath

Avoid putting a rug or carpet underneath a dining table. This is an area of the house where, like it or not, things somehow end up on the floor.

A flat surface it is much easier to keep clean and smelling fresh. You don't need to vacuum all the time, you can use a dustpan and brush.

If you want to find an old shrivelled pea you know where to look!

Furniture

Repair or mend furniture before buying new.

If you are unable to do this yourself find someone who can. If you have a friend who can do it perhaps return the favour with something else – offer to babysit in exchange for so many hours sewing or repairing the dining chair or table for example.

Before buying new, brighten rooms up with added soft furnishings like new cushion covers. That might be all that's needed. Or have a good clear out, clean and perhaps rearrange the furniture for a new look.

This is an opportunity to be creative at little cost.

Reading in comfort

Arrange the furniture so that if you read you will not need an extra light during the day in the winter. At night if you need a reading light on, turn the other main light off. *See more details in the energy section.*

Keeping the house cool

A few simple tips to keeping the house cool in summer. First, part-close curtains or draw blinds where direct sunlight shines on your windows to create as much shade in the house as possible.

Open windows at the same time to get air to circulate through to help keep the house cool and reduce stuffiness. Draw nets if you have them to keep any insects out across open windows or doors.

To be most effective do this at the beginning of the day before the house heats up. Think about extendible outside awnings or shutters. Do all this before thinking about buying fans or air conditioning.

Air conditioning

For those lucky people living in warm countries, your energy bills are about cooling the house not heating it.

If you have air conditioning, consider increasing the temperature dial by a few degrees.

Remember it is about reducing the heat in the home not making it cold. Turn air conditioning off in the rooms you don't use and keep the doors shut.

Dress in light sleeveless clothes if you have air conditioning on.

If you get cold or a stiff shoulder you know the room temperature is set too cold, so adjust the dial or turn it off for a while.

Alternatively try opening windows and closing the blinds to keep the sun out for a while.

Vacuuming or not?

If you have wooden, stone or laminate flooring you do not need to use the vacuum cleaner all the time. This saves in electricity and at times is quicker and easier to use a broom, dustpan and brush or mop instead as needed.

The contents of your vacuum cleaner can go on the compost heap, bag included if biodegradable, no need to put them in the black bin bag.

Dog/Pet smell

If you have a dog or other pet, the house can smell at times, so to avoid this, a few tips. Air the house a little bit more. Make sure you dry pets, including their feet when they come back in the house.

Your pet bird will enjoy a little wash too, so put a saucer or plate out somewhere safe in the house with a tiny amount of water (two tablespoons full) and let them have a splash about. Look up how to care for your pet if in doubt.

Damp dog smell is the worst. Give the dog a wash and shampoo and wash its bed/bedding in the washing machine

Dog/Pet smell
(continued)

regularly. Sprinkle the bed with bicarbonate of soda to neutralise odours.

Don't let dogs on the sofa, or if you do give them their own blanket and that can be washed regularly.

Fitted carpets are not ideal, wooden or tiled flooring is more suitable.

If you want to spray to mask the odour please use as a last resort and don't buy something especially. Just use up that old perfume you have around the house. Having more than one dog bed and alternatively airing or washing them is a good idea; and saves you time moving the bed around the house to suit your dog.

'Because you know your pet is worth it'

Yes I am at the beck and call of my dog!

Furniture polish

Instead of chemical products use olive oil instead; it works wonders. Use sparingly – a little goes a very long way.

Recycling made easy

Lounge and dining rooms usually don't need a bin. Take paper and recyclables to the downstairs recycling bins.

WEEE
Waste
Electrical
Electronic
Equipment

If you are replacing old TVs or other electrical equipment, recycle it, rather than sticking it in your black bag bin. The easiest thing to do is to take it to your local recycling centre where they take a variety of materials from households. Whenever you buy new electrical appliances, *the retailer is obliged* to either take back the old equipment in store for free or tell you where you can take it to recycle it for free.

Home collection may be offered, but stores are not obliged to do this, so may charge.

You can also find out where to recycle electrical equipment locally by looking on the council website or contacting them, or using the 'Bank Locator' search tool from Valpak. See link at the back of the book.

Home office

Principles
✓ Clean and tidy
✓ Bright and productive environment

Horrendous Household fact:
'On average a UK home spends between £45 - £80 a year powering electronic goods left in standby'
(*Energy Saving Trust, 2013*).

No matter if it's just a corner of the room for your personal records or if you're running a business from your home in a separate room, you can make the most of it. It is all about efficiency; be it time, space or reducing your consumption costs.

These ideas also apply to the work place and the tips start from how you get there.

Transport

If you go to work, think about alternatives to the car. What about a car share scheme? Or you could take the train or bus, or bicycle or walk if near enough.

Use the park and ride when you can, which saves on time you spend getting stuck in traffic. Cheaper or free parking might be available.

Positive view

Work in a room that gives you morning sun, so lighting can be kept to a minimum, and to enhance a productive working environment.

Face the window so you get the maximum amount of benefit from natural daylight. Have a blind instead of a curtain to let as much light in and also control glare from sunlight on your computer screen if necessary.

Keeping warm

It is possible in most homes to avoid having the heating on in the day. If working from home sitting at a desk, you can feel the cold that little bit sooner, so here are a few tips:

Put on more layers of thicker clothing. Ideally get out your winter sports thermals for a cosy under layer so you can still look professional on top. (I do not mean go put your coat, hat and gloves on)!

Lots of hot drinks help keep you warm and keep you moving so you will not stiffen up and reduce the chances of over straining your eyes.

In winter if you need the heating on turn down radiators in other rooms and keep the office door closed to keep the heat in.

Yet another cup of tea is my favourite!

A cuppa!

Only boil enough water for your mug, or use a flask and pour out a little at a time.

If your mug of tea has gone cold, no matter how little is left, microwave your tea instead of throwing it away and making a new cup. 20-25 seconds usually does it.

I use my microwave about 3-4 times a day to heat up my tea.

Printing

There's no need to print everything. Soft copies are fine and if important back them up. Decide what is best, depending on what it is. The less you print, the less paper and ink you need. You can save electricity and of course there's less dreaded filing.

Save paper

If you do need to print or photocopy use scrap paper first, especially for drafts.

Keep a spare ream of new A4 paper in the cupboard and load the printer tray with used paper only, that way you don't forget. Paper larger than A4 (such as A3) can be folded in half or cut to size.

Some magazines come in the post with an extra sheet of paper with just your address on it. This is ideal for your printer. Also some junk mail is not printed on all sides and again this can be used in the printer or for shopping lists and notepaper.

Keep all your junk mail and spare paper from old files you would bin and use them first as scrap paper. Most of the time you are printing for yourself and not sending a letter in the post or handing it to a client. You can also use lined paper in your printer by the way. Proof of purchase records from the internet can also be printed on scrap, as can e-tickets, car insurance forms and so on; you don't need good clean paper for that.

Save paper
(continued)

If you need to send out work on good clean paper, you can set your printer to print double sided or print the odd pages first and then feed back in to print the even pages on the back to save on the amount of paper used and postage costs.

Printer/ photocopier/ fax

Print in draft quality and black and white as much as possible.

To extend the life of your printer cartridge, take it out when the light comes on saying it is empty, give it a good shake and put back in. It might last a short while longer.

Recycle your printer cartridges. Usually your local shop will take them back and there might be a free post service. You can also get cash back online for some used cartridges so that's worth checking out before you get rid of them. That way they also go to a good home plus these sorts of chemicals are best recycled than binned, so please do your best.

Power down

Turn off all your electronics, not just the ones in the office. This includes computer screens as well as computers. Only turn printers on when needed. It is a waste to leave everything on standby and it's also a potential fire hazard. It can also extend the life of your equipment. For a typical home turning off standbys could save around £32 per year on energy bills (*E.On, 2013*).

Set all your computers and screen to turn off if not being used within one minute. You can do this in the settings. That way when someone gets distracted the computer is not on for no reason.

'Appliances left on standby can use as much as three quarters of the energy they use when they are fully switched on.' (*Affordable Warmth Network, 2013, p24*)

? DID YOU KNOW

'Household computers, printers, monitors and laptops on average make up around 13% of electricity around the home.' (Energy Saving Trust, 2013)

Mobile phones

Charge up during the day, you will be surprised what a few minutes can make and usually an hour or so does it, depending on your phone and how low it is. In the worst case it can take a couple of hours to charge from flat. Leave the charger in the home downstairs. Avoid charging up overnight to reduce circa 8 hours of unnecessary charging and electricity costs. Once fully charged, unplug the phone and the charger too.

To charge up even quicker, turn to airplane mode or off. This will reduce your ability to use the phone at the same time, but is a good tip to know if battery power is the key thing before you leave the house or while out and about.

Set up your smartphone to turn off if not being used within one minute. Lock your phone, not only for your safety, but to stop you accidently calling people from your pocket. You can do both in the settings.

Battery life is lost much quicker when there are several programs open. For an iPhone, for example, to close programs and apps, double click the home button then you'll see all the programs that are open. Tap and hold on the app then flick up and away to close each app.

This will save your battery life and save electricity bills as you are not charging the phone so much.

Most newer cell phones have lithium-ion batteries, while older ones generally have nickel-based batteries. Read the label on the back of the battery or in the technical specifications in the manual to determine which yours is.

Unlike Ni-Cd batteries, lithium-ion batteries' life is

Mobile phones *(continued)*	shortened every time you fully discharge them. Instead, charge them when the battery meter shows one bar left. Lithium-ion batteries, like most rechargeable batteries, have a set number of charges in them. *(WikiHow, 2013)* *Alternatively ask your in-house expert on all virtual matters – the teenager!*

Top tip for computers	Use an extension lead with an off switch. Plug all the PC, printer and speaker leads into the extension lead and when finished you need only turn off the extension lead at the switch. Make sure you don't add other equipment you hardly use, such as the fax or scanner. Just plug that in when needed and take out again.

Change search engine	It is believed a little energy can be saved by simply changing your search engine provider to a dark coloured background instead like Blackle.com *(Heap Media, 2013)*. It is easy to do and there's no cost involved, so it's worth a try.

New Computer	If an item is broken try to get it fixed first. There are now IT re-use companies that take your old computers and recondition them. If you're thinking about buying a new computer this is an opportunity for you to buy a second hand computer instead at a very modest price indeed. Ideal if you are not using the latest software or specialist programmes that take up loads of space on your computer, slowing it down. Ideal for home use too. Search online for second hand computers or see link at the back of the book in the bibliography section for one such company. If you are thinking about buying a new computer, a new laptop typically uses around 85% less energy than a new desktop computer. *(Energy Saving Trust, 2013)* and takes up less room too.

| Junk mail | Avoid getting junk mail by signing up to the mail preference service. You can do this online and is quick and easy (see link at the back of the book). Ideal for also registering previous occupiers to avoid getting their junk mail too. | |

| Post | If post arrives with plastic covers, use them as bin liners or poo bags for your pet. Cut off a corner and then cut along one side with a pair of scissors. Take out the contents and keep the bag.

Cut down on unnecessary posted subscriptions to magazines. A lot of information is now available online and is quick and easy to access. | |

| E-Cards | E-Cards are the new thing. There is no need to buy paper Christmas cards or birthday cards. You can send them by email and save money. You can donate the money saved to charity if you wish. Charities such as the Red Cross provide you with interactive themed cards too. Saves buying cards and postage. Just Google your favourite charity and see if they do any e-cards. | |

| Folders | Keep and reuse old ring binders, folders and plastic wallets. Usually a supply from your children will keep you in stock. Use them up before buying new. Just re-label them. | |

| Archives | When you run out of used paper for your printer, instead of grabbing for new paper pull out an old file or archive and have a clear out. Decide what you want to keep and what you can bin. Instead of binning all that paper put the paper only printed on one side in your printer, the rest you can put in the paper recycling bin or you might want to shed first if it contains confidential information. | |

Shredding

If you shred some of your paper you can still recycle it but it would be better to put it directly into a paper recycling bank, where it will go directly to the paper mills instead of a doorstep mixed collection scheme. Doorstep collection systems might get pre-sorted before they go to the paper mills, and shredded paper often gets rejected in these systems, as it is too fine. Banks usually go directly to the paper mills so this is avoided.

If you want to use the doorstep system use your paper box, if provided. Just put your shredded paper in a paper bag and fold it over to avoid it spilling out when processed. It is better to recycle it even if some is lost than all of it going in the waste bin.

Staples

Reduce the amount of staples you use and switch to paper clips which you can reuse.

You can also get staple-less staplers that puncture the paper.

Note pads

Use half used school exercise books. Remove the pages written on. Recycle if printed both sides, or use in the printer if written on just one side. The remaining exercise book is an ideal notebook.

Business Cards

Put the date you receive them on so you know how relevant or out of date they will become, or as is sometimes the case with me, they help you put a face to a name.

Use your own out of date business cards as shopping lists or 'post it' type prompt notes.

You can scan and store these electronically if you wish.

Books	Sell old books you don't need or have read online or donate them to charity shops. You can give magazines to your local doctors' surgery or charity shops.	
Envelopes	Save envelopes and reuse them by sticking over the address with a label and use a black marker to cover any unwanted franking marks. This means you do not need to buy envelopes. Keep all shapes and sizes and the padded ones too, as you never know when you'll need them. Recycle the ones you do not need in the paper recycling (unless they have bubble wrap in them).	
Scrap box	Have a scrap box of spare bits of ribbon, wrapping paper or gift cards, including any odd bits you can use to decorate your gifts. Having everything in one place makes it quick and easy and there's no need to rush out and buy some more.	
CDs and cases	Keep your old CD cases, as they will be useful elsewhere instead of buying more. Old CDs at present have limited use if you can't rewrite them. They make really good coasters or can be used in the garden to hang in the fruit trees or vegetable garden to deter birds.	
Printer cartridges	There are now various places where you can take your old cartridges for recycling and it really is best to do that as they contain chemicals that should be properly treated. Buying remanufactured cartridges from third parties if reputable are usually cheaper and for home use may be good enough, but make sure you can get your money back if not as these don't come cheap either. Some companies may buy or give you credit for your old used cartridges too, so investigate if that suits you.	

143

Reading glasses

Replace the lenses only. If you are replacing the frame and no longer need your glasses, donate them to your local opticians or directly to Vision Aid Overseas, see link at the back of the book.

Recycling made easy

The home office is probably the place where most paper ends up. So put your paper recycling box underneath the desk in the office area, inside the house. This makes life much easier. You can recycle all sorts of paper and even telephone directories.

You may need a small bin for general rubbish you can't recycle. Keep it in the office for convenience and then empty in the black bin outside when needed.

Also for the really keen, have an old small tin or similar in your desk draw for these odd bits of metal like paper clips, broken bits of metal, staples. You will be surprised how these bits add up. Metal is a very valuable resource and we should avoid losing it in a landfill. When passing the municipal recycling centre, drop it off.

Collect your used batteries in the same way and place in the battery recycling container at the recycling centre or local shop collection point.

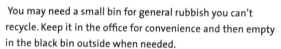

IT recycling

If an item is broken try to get it fixed first. There are now IT re-use companies that take your old computers and recondition them. Also various IT equipment can be sold online.

If that is not possible then it is best to recycle old IT equipment. There are a lot of metals inside that are best kept out of a landfill and are also very worthwhile to recycle.

Be careful when selling or disposing of computers, as you risk your personal data being misused. Always wipe your private data even if giving to a professional to recondition as above.

Garden

Principles

✓ In harmony with nature

Horrendous Household fact:
'Outdoor water use accounts for around 7% of the total water use, but in the summer this can rise to over 50% of peak demand.' (Waterwise, 2013).

If you have a garden and want to make use of your green fingers or are looking for a therapeutic hobby, all paths lead to plants and gardening be it a window box, patio or garden. The great thing about this hobby is, the amount of rewards you get far outweigh the costs. It's hard to quantify, but until you try to help a plant grow or grow something from seed you have no idea how much of a feelgood factor you get from it, not to mention some lovely apples or gorgeous rhubarb. Here are some ideas, which hopefully you are already doing or you might want to try.

Outside lighting

If you have external lights, then a sensor that turns them on when you approach will make them much cheaper to run than having them on all night on a timer or daylight sensor.

Fit energy saving light bulbs where you can. Halogen floodlights should only be on for short bursts and if left on can cost a small fortune. The Affordable Warmth Network suggest a 300W bulb may be sufficient, so try to replace your outside halogen lamp if you can.

What is the point?

One of the few things that are not necessary in a domestic setting are patio heaters. If it is that cold go in doors. Why waste energy and money heating the garden?

Blown away!

Gardeners have for centuries used the garden rake to collect leaves if wet or dry, which is still the best tool to use in your garden. Blowing them, if it works, just moves them to somewhere else and that's all. With no added benefit to the grass that raking brings and extra leaves in your borders are likely to smother tender plants this is more work not less. Leaves of course still need to be picked up too. Of course using a rake saves energy and money and is good for your garden.

Water butts

Water butts are great not only for watering the garden but for cleaning the car, cleaning the garden furniture, rinsing wellies and so on.

Make sure your water butt is clean and free from any debris. Ideally it should have a lid, this will stop things getting in, including sunlight to avoid any algae growing.

No water butt	If you do not have a water butt you can make your own or leave your bucket/wheelbarrow outside, you will be surprised how quickly it fills up. Or adapt your old plastic bin into a water butt. If you live in a climate where mosquitos are common, please ensure you follow proper guidelines and rules in your area.	
Grey water in the garden	You might be able to use some grey water for these jobs too. For cleaning out bins, washing the car, rinsing wellington boots and other things that don't need to be cleaned with fresh drinking water.	
Pets and water	With an empty bowl in the sink rinse out the pet water container and refill with fresh water. The water remaining in the bowl is 'grey' water and can be used elsewhere in the house and garden as highlighted in various places in the book.	
You don't need a hose	Use water from the water butt first. When the butt is empty use a bucket and fill from the tap instead of using a hose as you will use less water this way.	
The Car	Use the water butt water to clean your car. This will save you time, as you will not need to leather dry, as it leaves no smears. Clean your car as normal and use car shampoo with water butt water and then rinse with just water butt water, no need to dry or anything. Amazing! Occasionally when there is a drought be proud to do your bit	

The Car *(continued)*	and leave your car unwashed during this time. You will need to water butt for your plants then too. *This is a really handy tip; it saves me loads of time with amazing results!*	
Washing outside	If washing down garden furniture or a bike for example, do it outside outside on the grass (when the sun has gone in the summer) without using detergent. It helps water the grass and surrounding plants at the same time.	
Prune	Make sure that your garden plants are well pruned near your windows so they do not reduce the light coming into your rooms. This helps reduce the need for lights and heating in our UK climate. It also makes the room look much bigger and brighter.	
Watering plants	Plants prefer rainwater to tap water, so use your water butt water for your garden needs and for your house plants first. This saves you paying to water the garden. Get yourself a water butt or make your own. Avoid watering plants and the lawn from the tap or with a hose. If you do have a hose attach a spring loaded nozzle to cut of water supply quickly. Water plants around the roots (not leaves) in the early evening when the sun has gone down or early in the morning to reduce water evaporation. Wood chip and other mulches will help keep the water in. Instead of a little often, water well and less often this way roots will develop deeper in the soil, which will help the plant to thrive.	

Killing Weeds	Whenever you empty the kettle make it work. Poor left over boiling water on weeds in the patio to kill them.	
No need for sprinkler	Avoid using a sprinkler. Established plants in the garden should not need watering, so only do the sensitive plants and/or the fruit-bearing ones.	
Fruit	Make the most of your fruit trees or plants. If you don't have any, plant some. Use as much as possible, eat, juice up, cook, freeze or give away. Don't forget you can also harvest fruit from the forest; you will be surprised how many blackberries you can find at harvest time. *I once found raspberries in the forest too. Yum, yum!*	
Flower displays in the home	If you have a garden, however small, instead of buying flowers or to bulk out bought flowers use prunings from the garden, to add greenery to your flowers or have a green display. This makes the display look much more impressive or allows you to split the flowers into two vases. Put flowers on the compost heap when they are past their best. If you have green fingers, try growing from cuttings and seeds.	

Plant food

The best plant food is worm tea from my wormery and of course it is absolutely free, great for my indoor plants such as orchids and lillies and good for the garden too. To find out more search online to make your own wormery or see back of book for this link. (*Wiggly Wigglers, 2013*).

For fresh-cut flowers add 1.5 teaspoons of sugar and one tablespoon of white vinegar per pint of warm water. The sugar feeds the stems and the vinegar restricts the growth of bacteria.

Soil

Instead of buying topsoil use your own from your compost heap. Remember as well as your green garden waste add all your kitchen peelings, tea bags and coffee grounds daily or use a kitchen caddy. Once your compost is ready, put a pile in a wheelbarrow and break it up with a spade and mix before using in the garden. See below on how to make your own compost.

Lawns

Don't worry about established lawns turning brown in temperate climates like the UK. When the rain comes your grass will soon be green once more. Thames Water agrees and suggests letting lawns grow a little longer, especially in periods of drought, this will send down deeper roots and will help maintain a green lawn. (*Thames Water, 2013*)

If cutting lawns, leave the clippings on the lawn if they are short (1.5 – 2.5cm) during the main growing season. As they decompose, they release up to 30 per cent of the lawn's required nutrients. Remove clippings at all other times when decomposition is slow. (*BBC, Gardening basics, 2013*)

Grow your own

Grow your own fruit, veg and herbs if you can. Growing your own food can be a lot of fun for all the family as well as saving you loads of money and food miles. You can find out more about growing your own food, including when to plant,

Grow your own
(continued)

on the BBC Gardening website. *(BBC, Gardening basics, 2013)*

A food mile is a term that refers to the distance food is transported, from the time of its production until it reaches the consumer. Food miles are one factor used when assessing the environmental impact of food, including the impact on global warming. Without a doubt home-grown food ticks all the green boxes.

Food grown at home is also said to be tastier and higher in vitamins than shop-bought alternatives, and certainly you can't buy fresher. With home grown food you know it hasn't got pesticides or other toxins in, or you know exactly what and how much you have used.

Do read the label carefully if you buy bug repellents etc.

Can't wait till the goose-berries are ready – yum, yum.!

Growing from seed

No need to buy pots. Just use old small plastic yoghurt pots or similar to put your seeds in along with your compost and an old empty plastic bottle (with a few holes in) as your mini greenhouse – this a great way to speed up germination and keep nibbling pests away.

You can also you a paper potter to plant your seed in, just wrap a piece of scrap paper or card 10cm deep around an rolling pin leaving 3cms over the edge to fold under to make a pot. No need to de-pot too.

Potpourri

Collect and use old rose petals, along with any lavender or similar sweet smelling herbs from the garden to make your own potpourri. Add dried citrus peel to the mix. There are various receipts to follow or you can make up your own. Pick the roses that have scent, the others will just add colour and bulk and no more.

You can also put citrus peel like oranges and lemons on a saucer to deodorize various rooms.

Old CDs

Old CDs, if you can't rewrite them, at present have limited use. String them up in the garden in the fruit trees or the vegetable patch to deter birds.

No garden

You don't need to have a garden. You can grow herbs and small plants in window boxes; put containers on the patio too.

Don't forget you may be able to apply for an allotment with your local council. Rent prices vary depending on location and size of plot and there may be a waiting list so get your name down early.

See land share options below.

Land share

There may be a land share scheme near you. Find out online or ask your local council, as they may have details of one near you.

Land share brings together people who have a passion for home grown food, connecting those who have land to share with those who need land for cultivating food.

It's for people who:

- Want to grow their own fruit and veg but don't have anywhere to do it

- Have a spare bit of land they're prepared to share

- Can help in some way – from sharing knowledge and lending tools to helping out on the plot itself

- Support the idea of freeing up more land for growing

- Are already growing and want to join in the community.

For further details see their website details at the back of the book.

Plants

Choose plants that are native or suited to the local environment. That way they are more likely to thrive and will need less watering.

If a plant is not doing well it might be that it is in the wrong position. If so, dig up and move to a more suitable spot before it is too late. There are loads of tips online. Just type in the name of the type of plant to find out when and where to move it.

Established native trees and shrubs generally have such wide ranging roots that you do not need to water them.

(*Thames Water, 2013*)

Bee Happy

As you may know bees are having a tough time at the moment, and without them we will have serious problems in our food supply, as they are the world's pollinators. One in three mouthfuls we eat depend on pollination! (*The British Beekeepers Association, 2013*).

So plant bee-friendly flowers, don't get rid of all the wild flowers you have in the garden, let the grass grow and perhaps make a bee hotel out of left over bits of bamboo and twigs. A good idea if you are growing fruit and vegetables too. For more ideas see the British Beekeepers website details at the back.

Garden pests

Instead of going for the bought chemicals try some home remedies that are kinder to the environment and your purse. Such as controlling slugs by adding some sweet liquid like stale beer to a jam jar sunk into the ground.

Go bananas with aphids

Readers Digest (2013) article *Extraordinary Uses for Bananas* says "You can use bits of banana peel to get rid of aphids. Dig in, in small bits, around susceptible plants."

Bananas are also a good source of plant food if you don't have a compost heap.

Old plastic bags with air holes	Price stickers and fruit and veg stickers can be used to cover any holes in your old plastic bags. You can use the bags then for your compost bin caddy.	

Poo bags

No need to buy new bags, just save some plastic bags without holes and take with you on your walk. Do make sure the plastic bag has no holes or cover any holes in the plastic bag as above, a must for poo bags.

To avoid dog poo remaining in a plastic bag for years in a landfill, I take them home and empty the dog poo in an out of the way spot such as under a hawthorn hedge at the back of the garden and cover with soil and leaves to speed up decomposition. Put the used bag in the bin.

You can also put dog poo in the bin, but I think the most planet friendly way is under the hedge away from kids and the fruit and vegetable patch.

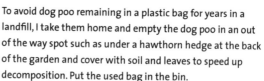

Make your own compost

Start a compost heap in the garden and before you know it you have your own compost for your garden and house plants.

With or without a compost bin, start a pile with twigs and dry leaves ideally on soil or lawn, then layer with any 'greens' you have (grass cuttings and uncooked fruit and veg, tea and coffee grounds from your kitchen peelings bin) and then a layer of any browns you have (twigs, dry leaves, shredded paper, animal bedding, hoover bag with contents) and keep on layering – the more you add, the quicker the pile heats up and the quicker you have compost. Typically this takes 6-9 months.

The hotter the climate the quicker you have finished compost. Layering speeds up this process too. No matter how much care you take with the compost heap it will compost down eventually no matter what, so give it a go and keep adding, don't wait to see compost before you add more. Once ready it will look like moist soil, crumbly and dark with some twiggy bits.

Make your own compost
(continued)

Home composting adds fertility to your soil and improves soil structure for free. It reduces the need to water and encourages healthy plant growth and provides food for growing plants. (*Buckinghamshire Local Authorities' Guide to Easy Home Composting, 2012*). **Making your own compost avoids having to buy chemical fertilizers.**

Once you are ready to use it, just put a spade or two in a wheelbarrow, remove any stones you see and use your spade to break up and roughly mix before putting around your plants and/or forking in. If using in containers, mix two parts compost to two parts ordinary soil from the garden, or if planting out from a pot top up with compost aiming for a 50/50 ratio of compost to soil.

If you need to buy compost, make sure you buy recycled garden waste compost. You will probably be able to buy this from your council at the local household waste recycling sites, garden centres and some DIY stores.

Green Cones

You can install Green Cones in your garden and as well as fruit and vegetable peelings and tea and coffee grounds they can take all your kitchen food waste. The advantage of this is that you have no smelly waste in your black bag bin, a real plus in summer. Also there is next to no maintenance once installed. Collect all food scraps, cooked and uncooked, mouldy or not, such as raw meat trimmings, bones, flour, bread, sauce, food scraps from plates, sinks and worktops; in fact any food including things you would not put on the compost bin. Just tip into the green cone and close the lid. It does not produce a compost you remove to use elsewhere; it feeds the ground around it from underground. It also works perfectly well without you adding what you can put on the compost heap i.e. uncooked fruit and vegetables. This makes it ideal for keen gardeners and larger families as you can have both the compost bin and green cone working to their optimum, with no smelly waste bins. If you want, you can add a little sprinkle of activator (powder) to keep things going if you are filling it a lot in winter,

Green Cones
(continued)

which you might like to do if you are putting a few big bird carcasses in as I do around Christmas time. Amazingly it all just disappears over time and there is no smell. To find out more see back of book for the link. (*Great Green Systems, 2014*)

I love my green cone.

Wormery

A wormery is a great addition and great fun for all the family if you have limited space and garden equipment and using a spade is not for you. You can make your own or buy. It is a bit like having a toy compost heap. The advantages are that it can be very small, ideal for a cottage garden or patio. The normal size is about the same as a big plant pot on legs.

It takes uncooked fruit and veg and garden waste and produces a liquid feed and a very fine moist compost material, both of which are great for plants inside and outside and saves you buying soil or plant food. All you need is worms. They eat everything up and the casts (the digested remains) are the compost.

Like all pets, it does require a bit of TLC, but the compost is amazing quality with no digging required. Simple rules to remember, do not let them get too hot – so keep them out of the hot sun in summer and maybe in the garage or shed in winter. You have to remember to feed them but they can go for a few weeks without a top up especially in cold weather.

To find out more see back of book for the link.

(*Wiggly Wigglers, 2013*)

Chickens

There is something idyllic about collecting your own eggs from your pet hens. The reality for most of us including me is that it sounds a nice idea but it's not quite so simple. That said, if you have the appropriate space and the desire having your own chickens will save you money, so I am told. To find out more I attach a link at the back of the book for those that might want to explore further.

Good deeds and ideas with the environment in mind

Principles

✓ Doing your bit for the environment

✓ Doing your bit for the community

✓ A fair future

A global view of giving:

*'The World Giving Index score is based on an average of three measures of giving behaviour - the percentage of people who in a typical month **donate money to charity, volunteer their time**, and **help a stranger**.'*

The 2014 report shows 'that giving is more than just about wealth, with only five G20 countries represented in the World Giving Index Top 20 – indeed, eleven G20 countries are even ranked outside of the WGI Top 50.' (Charities Aid Foundation, 2015).

As well as saving pounds and the planet you can also do things where the only gain is that warm comfortable feeling in your tummy that you get when you've done the right thing. This is not to be ignored—doing something for someone else will make you feel good, and that is good for your mental health and happiness, so you do gain a benefit after all.

Below are some ideas that help the planet along the way too.

The charity shop	Donate all your unwanted items you don't want to sell to your local charity shop who will put them to good use. You can also support your local charity and have a go and buy second-hand clothing or products where possible.	
Unwanted Jewellery	For all those odd earrings or broken necklaces and bracelets instead of binning them, give to a worthy cause for a second lease of life. Search online or check with your local charity shop or send to old Jewellery appeal from the Alzheimer's Society with a freepost jiffy bag see link at the back of the book.	
Donate on-line	Use a website such as Freecycle, which is made up of over 5,000 groups with over 7 million members around the world. It's a grassroots and entirely not for profit movement of people who are giving (and getting) stuff for free in their own towns. It's all about reuse and keeping good stuff out of landfills. (*The Freecycle Network, 2013*) See link at the back of the book.	
Spare paint	Instead of leaving those unused tins of paint to go off with age, donate them to charity where they can be put to better use. Find out where the nearest Community Repaint scheme is and clear those tins out of the garage. Alternatively your local council may provide a collection and reuse service for worthy causes. See link at the back of the book.	
Magazines	Only going to read it once? Give to surgeries or other waiting rooms or the local charity shop.	

Unused stuff

Finished with it? Give it a second life. Instead of slinging it in the bin, take it to a charity shop or your local household waste site if you can't sell it at a car boot or online.

Volunteering

Helping out at a charity shop is a good idea if you have some spare time, want to get out of the house, do something worthwhile and meet some new people.

For a quick and easy way to find out what local charity work opportunities exist, check out an organisation called Do-It. They make it easy to find out what's available in your area and help choose what to do. Just punch in your postcode and scroll through the options. See link at the back of the book.

An ideal alternative to retail therapy for lifting your spirits.

Recycle

Separate all your recyclables for the greater good. You can recycle paper, card, glass, metal cans and plastic bottles easily. The local council can pick almost all of these up from your doorstep. Some Councils collect green garden waste, food waste, plastic packaging such as plastic food trays and tubs, textiles and batteries.

There are also likely to be household waste recycling sites in your area. These now take a huge variety of things that will get recycled, including electrical goods, metals, old furniture, rubble, soil, wood, used cooking oil, paint, batteries and so on. The recycle-more website has a bank locator so it is easy to find what is near you. See link at the back of the book.

Buy recycled

Buy recycled and environmental friendly products when you can. There are a multitude of products out there from clothes and your weekly newspaper to fence posts.

Fair trade	Buy more Fairtrade goods. Fairtrade is a tool for development that ensures disadvantaged farmers and workers in developing countries get a better deal through the use of the international FAIRTRADE Mark. See link at the back of the book.
Freedom foods	Freedom Food is the only UK assurance and food labelling scheme dedicated solely to improving farm animal welfare. See link at the back of the book.
Buy local	Support your local businesses and food growers by buying local when you can.
Less chemicals	Avoid over-coloured or bleached foods when you can, such as refined sugar. This whitened sugar has become the norm in supermarkets but now at last some are stocking natural unrefined cane sugar, which is light golden in colour and not to be confused with brown sugar. Refining sugar removes all of sugar cane's natural minerals and nutrients, which remain present in unrefined sugar. These include phosphorus, calcium, iron, magnesium and potassium. (*ehow, 2013*)
Textiles	Choose textile products made with the lowest energy and toxic emissions if you can. Also take into consideration good information on labour standards. For further information search ethical clothing online, see link at the back of the book for Fashion-conscience.com.

Wrapping paper	Buy only paper, not foil wrapping paper, so you can recycle.	

Presents	For presents, offer promises instead of buying things – such as babysitting gift vouchers in return for gardening duties. You can do a secret Santa version if you wish. Choose consumable presents that you can buy or make yourself, like cakes, or productive ones like a herb window box or a vegetable seed set, a voucher or a pressure cooker, which helps lower bills in the short or long term. Alternatively you could donate to a charity as a 'good gift' like sponsoring an animal at a zoo or providing a chicken to feed a family in Africa. An example is goodgifts.org, who offer shoe-box present for orphans. Hire clothes for special occasions instead of buying, or borrow.	

Go crackers	Make your own crackers from left over wrapping paper and toilet rolls and fill with sweets or other gifts and add a joke if you wish. Or make from material and reuse each year. If you are really creative you can make Xmas napkins and tie with ribbon around the toilet roll and fill as above. Therefore you have a table decoration, cracker and napkin all in one that you can reuse each year. I tend to have different themes for the gifts each year for my crackers. Initially I used to save all appropriate promotional gifts throughout the year and then use them to fill the crackers. From key fobs to skin care samples, these are all much more popular than the bought crackers.	

Gift tags	Make your own gift tags from last year's Christmas cards. Send e-cards. Reuse your wrapping paper or bags if you can.	
Get creative	For inspiration go on line to get ideas on how to get creative a good place to search online at Pinterest.	

Energy

Principles

✓ Turn it down

✓ Turn it off

Horrendous Household fact:

'Reducing our energy consumption will not only have a positive effect on the environment but will also help cut fuel bills and save money. UK households are responsible for over 30% of the total carbon dioxide which is emitted into the atmosphere.' (Act on Energy, 2014).

We all need and want power. Be it freedom of speech and general liberty or freedom to turn on! Both of which, when you have it, you take for granted – like a lot of things in life I suppose.

The fact is that generating enough electricity for the whole population 24/7 is a big problem, and ensuring we are self-sufficient as a country in terms of matching our needs with our production capabilities is not currently being achieved in the UK. Out of sight might be out of mind but at this time we are reliant on imports to keep the lights on!

A staggering 27% of the UK's CO_2 emissions come from the home when we use heat light and power (*Energy Saving Trust, 2005*). The biggest utility bill for the average home that has central heating is your energy bill. We use energy for heat, light, hot water and electricity for our various appliances. If you have ever had a power cut, you suddenly realise how much we use it and how much we waste it too. Simple changes can make a huge difference to your bills and a great contribution to reducing your impact on the planet without compromise to your quality of life. ***Taking steps to reduce your energy consumption and wastage is probably the single most important thing you can do for the environment. It is also the easiest way to save money, so what's stopping you?***

Grants, advice and Support

There are various grants, advice and support out there to make your home more energy efficient, and you will be surprised to find out how much could be free. This applies even if you are renting so find out what's available from your local council. Things covered could range from an energy savings check, loft insulation, boilers, wall insulation and draught-proofing. These offers may vary over time so make sure you don't miss out.

Loft insulation

In terms of reducing your heating bills, insulating your loft or flat roof is one of the easiest things to do, and you can do it yourself. It will save you wasting heat and therefore save you money on your fuel bills. It will pay for itself in about 2 years if you have no insulation at the moment.

'Heat rises, and in an un-insulated home a quarter of your heat is lost through the roof. (*Energy Saving Trust, 2014*)

If you already have insulation, check it is the recommended 27cms depth. Get your school ruler out and go check. If not, an insulation top up could save you money too.

If this is not an option, improvise. Keep things in the loft that help insulate it, such as spare cardboard moving house boxes, spare soft furnishings boxed, across the floor of the loft for example.

If you want to board out your loft and need to buy new, use insulating board.

Do keep your empty suitcases and Christmas décor, old toys and fancy dress you can't yet part with in the loft too. Added insulation in the loft equals free space in your cupboards. Useful to have, as you will need this cupboard space for all your new purchases on account of the savings you've made!

In between the rafters if you do not have any insulation and can't insulate in the normal way, you can add shredded paper or broken up bits of cork. Store your odd bits of wool too. You can use old pieces of wood/chip board to cover insulated bits of loft. Lay your boards across the rafters so you

Loft insulation
(continued)

can walk on them and store things on them, it all helps.

Remember air needs to circulate freely in the loft to keep the house dry and warm. Do be sensible with what you store in the loft – watch out for fire hazards or hoarding too much stuff. Avoid putting anything heavy in the loft too.

Wall insulation

About a third of all the heat lost in an un-insulated home goes through the walls *(Energy Saving Trust, 2014)*.

Insulating your cavity walls is therefore a worthwhile undertaking. Average payback times are three years or less. *(Energy Saving Trust, 2014)*.

Grants may be available in your local area so enquire with your local council.

Solid walls can have external or internal insulation installed and could save you around £270 on your fuel bills. *(Energy Saving Trust, 2014)*. Payback time is much longer as installation costs can be high depending on the level of work required.

Insulate

Draughts in the home are a drain on your heating bills. Draught-free homes are comfortable at lower temperatures – so you'll be able to turn down your thermostat and save money.

Put insulation tape around doors and windows where needed to cut down on draughts, and don't forget your letterbox.

Draught-proofing your home around doors and windows could save you on average £10 – £50 each year and could also save you another 10% on your heating bill. *(Energy Saving Trust, 2014)*.

There are various options on the market, which are discreet so you don't notice them. Don't forget all the other small holes around the house around pipes and wires leading outside, fill with filler or sealants and check out your local DIY store what you can do from gaps between floorboards to unused chimneys.

Be careful in areas that need good ventilation, such as where there are gas fires or rooms where a lot of moisture is produced.

Heating and hot water

Find the manuals for your boiler and hot water central heating system, if lost get hold of another one either online or from the supplier, whose details should be on the boiler, warm air systems, storage heaters or other heating appliances. Read the instructions to ensure you are getting the most out of the system you have. Having the settings at the optimum level will make it worthwhile and help reduce your heating bills. If renting, make sure you get a copy so you can manage heating and bills.

Boilers account for around 55% of what an average household spends in a year on energy bills, so an efficient boiler makes a big difference.

Replacing an old gas boiler with an A-rated high-efficiency condensing boiler and improving your heating controls ... could save you as much as £310 a year.' (*Enterprise Utilities, 2015*) If your boiler was installed before 2005 it really is worth checking out.

A jacket on your hot water tank (if you have one) is a cheap but effective way to lower bills and easy to do. If you have already got a jacket check it is 75mm+ thick, if not, it might be worth getting a new one. DIY cost for a jacket is about £15. The annual saving could be £20 to £35 each year and more if you heat your water electrically! If you have currently no jacket, installing one could save you around £85-£130 a year! (*Energy Saving Trust, 2014*)

Those with new boilers can lower their bills by installing a room thermostat. You can also get a programmable wireless one, which lets you choose the times and temperatures at which your central heating operates.

This means you're not wasting energy heating your home when you don't need to, so you can save on your heating bills. By using these clever thermostats, you can set your home temperature just the way you like it and it will automatically turn off your boiler once your home reaches the temperature you've set. Plus the thermostats are fully wireless, so you don't need to worry about having to hide cables or mains power.

Thermostatic radiator valves control how hot the radiator gets. So instead of all radiators being the same setting, you can regulate the temperature with a dial control - ideal for

Heating and hot water
(continued)

making sure the radiator in a room is at the correct temperature and not too cold or hot. You can fit these yourself onto the radiator. Depending on the fitting it might be a simple case of unscrewing and replacing with a new radiator valve or you may have to drain the system before installing and at this time the heating in the property will be off. There are also no-drain options too. You can do this yourself, if you're good at DIY. If you're not sure how to install or what sort of heating system you have, get advice or help to install before you begin.

If renting, just remember to keep everything you have removed off the radiator in a safe place, so when you leave the rented property you can remove your thermostatic radiator valve and replace with what was installed. Alternatively leave it with the property if you prefer. Depending on your arrangements with the landlord, it is always best to check before beginning any work.

'Installing and correctly using a room thermostat and thermostatic radiator valves could save £70-£150 a year.' (*Energy Saving Trust, 2014*)

Installing thermostatic radiator valves can cut around 10% from your heating bills. (*Carbon Trust, 2014*)

Have your boiler serviced once a year to ensure your boiler and heating system is working efficiently and safely.

A free annual service or safety check may be included with your supplier or maintenance contract so find out what's available.

Turn it down

Reduce the temperature of your radiators or central heating dial by 2 degrees or a little at a time. As the seasons change from winter to spring remember to adjust the timer to suit. 18°C to 21°C is ideal. Not all thermostats are accurate, so see how you go. Reducing your room temperature by 1°C could cut your heating bills by up to 10%, between the 18°C to 21°C. (*Affordable Warmth Network, 2013*)

If you have a timer, set your heating and hot water to come on only when required rather than all the time.

Turn it down *(continued)*	Turn down radiators in rooms not used much and close the door. Turn down your hot water temperature dial too. Your hot water thermostat should be set at 60°C/140°F. *(Act on Energy, 2013)* Tell-tale signs that your central heating is on too high is when you are wearing thin summer clothes, next to nothing, no socks or slippers and it is not the height of summer. If this is the case wear normal clothes and slippers and turn down the heat; not the other way round. Central heating when too hot has other drawbacks such as over-drying your skin. *(Chelsea and Westminster Hospital, 2014)* Before turning the heat up on your central heating system do check that all the radiators are getting warm all the way to the top and bleed radiators that are cold at the top. An ideal thing to check in autumn when the heating starts to get used again.	

Pipes	Insulate your hot water tank and boiler pipes including boiler pipes in the loft. Primary pipe insulation costs about £10 and saves about £10 each year on your energy bill *(Energy Saving Trust, 2014)*.	

Radiator insulation	Radiator reflector panels can be fitted behind radiators which reflect the heat back into the room and not the outside wall and aid convection, which is ideal for walls with no cavities i.e. solid brick walls or ones where there is no cavity wall insulation, but still a benefit whichever type of radiator you have with or without an insulated wall. You could potentially save up to 20% on your heating bills with radiator reflectors. *(Joulesave, 2014)*	

Don't waste heat

In winter turn off heating 30 minutes before you go to bed/ leave the house. The more insulated the house is, the earlier you can turn the central heating off, so set it to turn off a little earlier if you can.

Set the central heating timer to come on 30 minutes before you get up/come back from work. This time is approximate so you may need to adjust it according to your needs. Or just turn it on when you get up/come back from work, ideal if you do not have a set routine each day.

As the weather outside warms up, adjust the central heating timer to reflect this. For example set the clock to turn off an hour earlier in the morning and evening. Or turn the timer to off during the day on an ad-hoc basis while the weather is changeable. If you have thermostatic radiator valves turn these down or off too. Small changes can make big differences.

Good ventilation

A house that is too hot and stuffy allows germs to spread and live longer, especially on any damp surfaces, which could result in more colds and flu.

'Effective ventilation may also help keep bacteria, viruses and other pollutants out of the indoor air. Research shows that airflow and ventilation can affect how diseases spread indoors. The more stagnant the air is, the more likely diseases are to spread.' (*American Lung Association, 2013*)

Air vents

If you have air vents they are there for a reason, so do not block them. Appliances such as fridges and heaters need to breathe properly to work safely and efficiently. Likewise a kitchen and bathroom need to be ventilated to remove condensation and reduce/eliminate the formation of black mould. Remember to open the window before or after showering and keep the bathroom door closed until the condensation has gone. Alternatively if you can't open a window, use an extractor fan.

Air vents

If you add a lot of cold water to your shower/washing up, turn your hot water thermostat down. You are more likely to need to do this in the summer when the incoming tap water temperature is higher. A lot of boilers heat the water by a few degrees higher than the incoming tap water temperature so this makes a huge difference from winter to summer of the hot water temperature coming out of your tap.

With a 23kW boiler, at standard water flow rate:

Summer - typical mains incoming temp is 15°C, hot water temp will then be 50°C

Winter - typical mains temp is 4°C, hot water temp will then be 39°C (*H.C. Plumbing & Gas Services, 2013*).

If you have a hot water tank, as above, this should be set at 60°C (*Act on Energy, 2013*).

Make sure you look for the Energy Saving Trust Recommended label when you're buying heating controls – it's your guarantee that the product you're buying is the most energy efficient on the market and will help you to save money and energy, regardless of how old your boiler is.

Home Energy Check

There are various ways to check your energy consumption. To see how good you are at saving energy you can go online to the Energy Saving Trust's website and take the test! Also some other energy suppliers have their own versions. Go ahead and find out what you can save. See link at the back of the book.

Renewable energy

Check if you have or can opt for renewable energy from your electricity supplier and compare prices, it might be worth your while to change or switch to another supplier that gives you a better deal.

Renewable energy could come from a variety of sources such

Renewable energy
(continued)

as wind, sunlight, tides, waves and geothermal heat from underground. The big plus with renewable energy sources, as the name indicates, is that they do not run out.

Considering Solar power or other?

If you are thinking of generating your own energy and selling any surplus back to the national grid a few points to note.

In the UK, homes require (if being sold, rented or built) an Energy Performance Certificate (EPC), which rates the property, band A being the best.

To benefit from the higher rate feed-in tariff the property has to be between A – D to be eligible.

In short this means insulate your home properly before you consider solar panels. It also makes the most financial sense.

Turn off the standbys

My pet hate...

...Turn off all appliances at the socket when not in use. Any appliance on standby (you can usually see the tell-tale little light), uses some electricity which you are paying for. Chargers such as electric toothbrushes could still be using power even when fully charged.

Therefore once charged, turn off electric toothbrush, mobile, computer, screen, TV, speakers, video recorder and all those gadgets in the garage too. Some appliances might lose their time displays, so decide which ones you need on and which you don't. You will still be using some power to charge up unnecessarily or for it being on standby and will be charged for it for every single minute, so turn off at the socket where you can. An alternative is to buy a standby saver lead suitable for your computer or TV set up.

'A typical household can save between £45 and £80 a year just by remembering to turn off appliances left on standby.' (*Energy Saving Trust, 2015*)

| **Top tip for computers** | Use an extension lead with an off switch. Plug all the PC, printer and speaker leads for example in the extension lead and when finished you need only turn off the extension lead at the switch. Or if there's no switch on the extension, switch it off at the wall socket. | |

| **Go for cold** | Which tap you turn on at the sink is more of a habit most of the time than a conscious thought. So to avoid wasting energy check you automatically go for the cold tap (unless you need hot water) or make a conscious effort to switch to cold as a general rule, when you can. If you are turning the tap on for only a couple of seconds, the hot water will not reach you in that short space of time so go for cold instead. | |

| **Boil just enough** | Just boil enough water in the kettle for what you need (remember to ensure you cover the element). Use spare hot water wisely before it cools. Soak pots in sink or clean out the pedal bin or pour on weeds in the patio instead of using chemicals. |  |

| **Need hot water?** | If boiling vegetables, heat water in the kettle first then add to the pan (*uswitch, 2014*). It's quicker than boiling water in the pan and more energy efficient. Put a lid on the pan, (*uswitch, 2014*). This way you can use less water, less energy, and save on cooking time. | |

Steaming

Steaming vegetables *(uswitch, 2014)* is good. Steaming uses less water and energy and will cook more quickly. Also more vitamins will remain in the food. Use your normal pans and just buy a simple colander, add water in the base of the pan put vegetables in the colander and put the lid back on.

Cooking

Set the temperature dial to the temperature you want and not higher (it will not heat up any more quickly). *(Affordable Warmth Network, 2013)*

Avoid opening the oven door while cooking. When using the oven make the most of it and cook various dishes such as desserts and vegetables at the same time as well as the roast dinner.

If you have a small upper-level oven, use that when you have smaller or fewer items. Fan ovens use about 20% less electricity than conventional ovens. *(Affordable Warmth Network, 2013)*

Turn the oven and hob off a little before cooking has finished. Once you are finished with the oven you can warm your plates before serving so the dinner will keep warmer for longer. Thereafter you can leave the oven door open to allow the heat (and the yummy scent of apple pie or roast dinner) to enter the room.

Cooking in bulk and freezing is a good way of saving time and energy.

Pots and pans

Use the right sized pot for the volume of food to be cooked and keep the lid on.

Cook with the right sized heating element – i.e. one that's the same size or smaller than the pot – to ensure it heats the pot from underneath and nothing is wasted heating around the outside of the pot.

Turn the heat down once you have reached the correct temperature to simmer and put the lid back on, keep an eye

Pots and pans
(continued)

on the pot to make sure it does not boil over and it is still cooking as you wish, and keep reducing the temperature setting if you can.

With the lid on, using an electric hob for example, once boiling point has been reached you can maintain the cooking process and should be able to reduce the heat by up to about a third. This saves energy compared to boiling with the lid off at a higher power level!

Cut the food down into smaller, even-sized pieces and it will be ready quicker too. This way of boiling also uses less water with a lid and cooks quicker at a lower temperature, as the heat is not lost and water does not evaporate.

Overcooking your vegetables is also less nutritious as you lose some vitamins and minerals. Institute for Optimum Nutrition (1992).

Steam and pressure cook

This saves energy, water and time compared to conventional boiling, cooking or using an oven.

Microwave

This is a quick and easy way of cooking things, and is also very energy efficient. Instead of turning on another ring or putting the oven on, maybe the microwave will do the job just as well. Ideal for reheating your half-drunk cup of tea (20 seconds does it). Also for cooking vegetables, meat and fish, making custard and heating up last night's leftovers for lunch and much more.

Typical energy savings range from 21% – 81% depending on what you are cooking. Heating a ready meal in the microwave instead of using the oven could save 55-73% energy. (*Association of Manufacturers of Domestic Appliances, 2014*)

Fridge

Refrigerators should be kept between 0°C to 4°C.

Use a fridge thermometer to ensure it is at the right temperature. 'A fridge that is 10 degrees colder than necessary can use 25 per cent more energy.' (*California Energy Commission, 2014*)

An almost full fridge uses less energy than an empty one, (California Energy Commission, 2014) so stock up on items and aim to keep your fridge about three quarters full.

If your fridge is nearly empty, remember you can put your jam and chutneys in glass jars in the fridge too. If not yet opened put them at the back behind the open pot. Also to ensure you have chilled drinking water to hand, put a jug freshly filled each day in the fridge to use as you need. Not only convenient and energy efficient, but improved taste.

If running low you can store water-filled containers inside. The mass of cold items will enable the fridge to recover more quickly after the door has been opened. Remember not to overfill it, since that will interfere with the circulation of cold air inside.

Freezer

An almost full freezer uses less energy to keep cold than an empty one, (*California Energy Commission, 2014*) so stock up on items and aim to keep about three quarters full.

When you have space, that's the time to debug the soft toys by first putting them in a plastic bag and then in the freezer. Of course also a great opportunity to make dinner for 4 and freeze half for a quick meal another day.

Running a freezer at a colder temperature than necessary will use more energy and therefore cost more to run.

Freezers should be kept at -18°C to -25°C. Use a fridge thermometer to ensure it is at the right temperature.

If running low you can store water-filled containers inside, ice cube trays and so on. The mass of cold items will enable the freezer to recover more quickly after the door has been opened. On the other hand, don't overfill it, since that will interfere with the circulation of cold air inside.

Buying a Fridge or Freezer

If you're buying a new fridge or freezer, there are now frost-free versions, but these have mixed reviews and at the moment consume more energy as a rule. There are various styles – chest, upright, combined or separate fridge and freezer – all of which have varying running costs. Check the energy ratings for each before buying, as some appliances could cost you around £25 to run a year and some over £87 (*Which? 2014*).

So check out the energy rating label first to work out the total real cost to you or use Which? It has handy online calculator. See link in the reference section.

Typically you could save £57 in energy bills on an A+ rated fridge freezer over the market average over the lifetime of the product. (*Energy Saving Trust, 2015*).

See example energy label.

Freezer maintenance

Avoid putting the appliance next to a heat source such as a radiator or cooker or in direct sunlight.

An iced up freezer does not run as efficiently, so make sure you defrost it regularly.

Make sure air can circulate around the condenser coils by leaving a space between the wall and the appliance of at least 3cms. Keep your refrigerator coils clean. (*California Energy Commission, 2014*)

Check door seals to make sure they are airtight. To test them, close the door on a piece of paper and try to pull it out. If the paper slides out easily, you're wasting energy and money by letting cold air leak out!

Dishwasher

Stack the dishwasher full before putting it on.

If there is no burnt-on food, or if your dishes have been pre-rinsed in the sink, use a lower setting, which skips pre-rinsing it again. Saves time and energy and gives you less wear on your washing machine.

Pre-rinse everything in grey water in your bowl before stacking in the dishwasher. A good habit to get into to ensure nothing bakes on and ideal if you don't fill the dishwasher every day.

Choose an energy efficient dishwasher. Energy costs can range from as little as £22 a year to £68 (*Which? 2014*).

On average you could save around £12 a year on running costs with a new dishwasher compared to an old inefficient machine of the same size, as well as using less water.
(*Energy Saving Trust, 2015*)

Washing machines

An energy efficient washing machine will save you money on your electricity bill. (*Energy Saving Trust, 2015*).

Wash your clothes on a programme with a lower temperature and make sure each wash load is full to reduce the amount of washing you do.

Modern washing powders and liquids now work just as well on lower temperatures.

Washing clothes at 30 degrees instead of a higher temperature uses around 40% less energy. See link to (*Which, 2015*)

A full load in your washing machine uses half the water of two small loads. (*Thames Water, 2014*) If that means you don't use the spin cycle to save doing a separate wash, that's what you do.

Spin your clothes in the washing machine on the highest spin cycle to remove as much water as possible. The washing machine consumes less energy on the spin cycle compared to the dryer. This means clothes will dry quicker too with less need for line drying or the tumble dryer.

Don't spin If you can

Hang your clothes to dry on the line outside and/or use a clotheshorse inside. Some shirts can be dried straight on ahanger. This will save on ironing. It's best to have an airier hanging from the ceiling or wall over the bath or in a utility room. It's quick, easy and convenient. Or you might have an airing cupboard you can use.

Lighting

Turn off lights when leaving a room or not using it. You will ALWAYS save energy if you turn the light out when you leave the room, whatever type of lights you have, even if it's only for a minute or two. (*Energy Saving Trust, 2015*)

Replace bulbs with low energy ones both inside and outside the house. Pay extra attention if buying bulbs which are connected to a dimmer switch, as not all are compatible!

Think before you turn the light on, a desk light or reading light may be better than overhead central lighting. Halls and landing lights are usually left on for various reasons so fit a motion sensor light switch or time delay switch that you push in and it turns the light off after a minute or so. You can buy these at any good DIY store.

If you replace a traditional light bulb with an energy saving light bulb such as a compact fluorescent bulb (CFL) of the same brightness you will typically save around £3 per year. (*Energy Saving Trust, 2015*). Don't forget to use the lowest wattage you need too.

LED lights are good for replacing spotlights and dimmable lights. They are more expensive to buy but well worth it as they are more efficient than CFLs and will save you money in the long run. Check light bulbs are compatible with a dimmer switch.

If replacing halogen down-lighters in your home, 'LEDs are an excellent energy efficient alternative.' (*Energy Saving Trust, 2015*)

CFL bulbs can also last up to 10 times longer than filament ones and use about 75 – 80% less electricity than a filament bulb. (*Energy Saving Trust, 2015*)

Having a range of lights in a room, all with separate switches, will make it easier to achieve the lighting you want and need, whenever and wherever you want it.

DID YOU KNOW

'Lighting accounts for 7% of a typical household's energy bills and cutting your lighting bill is one of the easiest ways to save energy and money in the home.(

Energy Saving Trust, 2013)

Timed light switches

Timed light switches might be a good option. They turn off in a couple of minutes if using a pressure switch. These are ideal for the hall/landing and are cheap and easy to install.

Motion sensor lights detect motion so come on and then turn off after a minute if they sense no movement. Either option is ideal for the hall. You could also investigate where else in the house you could fit these sensors. There are various on the market and prices start from around £15 each.

Outdoor lighting

If you have external lights, then a sensor that turns them on when you approach will make them much cheaper to run than having them on all night on a timer or daylight sensor.

Fit energy saving light bulbs where you can. Halogen floodlights should only be on for short bursts and if left on can cost a small fortune (*Affordable Warmth Network, 2013*).

Energy Saving Trust Mark

If buying new or second hand equipment, make sure it has the energy saving trust logo on it and check the rating. Choose ideally an A+++ rating for the most energy efficient. You can work out the whole cost to run the appliance as well as buying it, to make sure you get the best overall deal. Read the small print to find out what the running costs will be and compare before you buy.

Light on in the day?

You should not need to put lights on in the day. Open curtains and nets fully. Perhaps you need to rearrange the furniture, so you do not have your back to the window when working for example. Bring the dining table nearer the window. Put big, tall furniture in the dark corners of the room away from the main windows.

If working from home have the desk next to the window looking out. A louver blind works better than curtains as you can adjust the light coming in as needed and helps with glare when working on a computer.

Let the heat/light in

Open curtains fully to let as much light in as possible. When fitting curtain tracks make sure there is enough space for the curtains to sit back from the window when not drawn.

If you are away at work all day do not be tempted to close the curtains hoping to stop the heat escaping. You are losing more by stopping the sunlight coming in and also not helping any potential damp problems, which will make you feel even colder.

Make the most of the light

Trim outside plants back or move them so they do not obstruct the light coming into the room from the window. Make sure windows are clean and keep big items of furniture away from windows so they don't block any light.

All these things will make the room darker, colder and feel smaller.

Windows

Windows could lose around 25% of your heat for the average home with single glazing and this could be reduced to only 12% with standard double-glazing or even down to 8% with low emissivity glass. Double glazing can reduce noise between 17 and 37%. (*Glass & Glazing Federation (2014)*).

When replacing windows, start with the rooms that you heat the most such as the downstairs lounge, a useful tip if you don't want to do the whole house in one go.

Windows
(continued)

Window Energy Ratings use a consumer friendly traffic light style A-E ratings guide similar to that used on 'white' goods *(such as fridges, freezers and washing machines).*

You can use this ratings label to make more informed choices about the energy efficiency of the windows you are looking to purchase.

Replacing all windows, which are single glazed, in a typical semi with A-rated double-glazing you could save around £90 - £120 each year on your energy bills *(Energy Saving Trust, 2015).*

Keep the heat where you want it

Keep doors to rooms shut when appropriate. This stops the heat moving into these unused spaces. It also helps you regulate the thermostats on the radiators more effectively. At night when everyone is home with children and perhaps pets too, this might not be practical all the time, but do what you can with as many rooms as possible.

Let the heat out

Drying clothes directly on the radiators should be avoided. Your boiler will need to work harder than it needs to *(British Gas, 2013).* Put a clotheshorse near to the radiator instead. This will help dry clothes and let the radiator heat the room at the same time.

Keep the cold out

At dusk close all nets and curtains to keep the heat in (and the bugs out). Remember to close internal doors whenever possible. Heavy and/or lined curtains with an enclosed pelmet are best. Place wardrobes and big furniture on outside walls of a room if possible.

Airing the house	In cold weather just air the bedrooms for 10 minutes at around the hottest time of day (lunch time). Do not heat the house at this time.	

Dress accordingly	If you are sitting for long periods of time in the house in cold weather – working from home, for example – or reading and watching TV during the day when the heating is usually off, put on another layer like a wool jumper or if you get cold feet, warm socks or tights under trousers before you turn the heating on or up. Making a hot drink is also a great idea and helps you rest your eyes from the screen or book and stretch your legs a bit too. If you are still cold after half an hour put the heating on. It is important for the very young and old to stay warm, so please bear that in mind.	

Keep cool	Depending where you live and the time of year, avoid buying air conditioning or fans or reduce their use.	

Air conditioning	For those lucky people living in warm countries, your energy bills are about cooling the house not heating it. If you have air conditioning, consider increasing the temperature dial by a few degrees. Remember it is about reducing the heat in the home not making it cold. Turn air conditioning off in the rooms you don't use and keep the doors shut. Dress in light sleeveless clothes if you have air conditioning on. If you get cold or a stiff shoulder you know the room temperature is set too cold, so adjust the dial or turn it off for a while. Alternatively try opening windows and closing the blinds to keep the sun out for a while.	

A simple way to keeping the house cool in summer

Part-close curtains/draw blinds where direct sunlight shines on your windows to create as much shade in the house as possible. Open windows at the same time to get air to circulate through to help keep the house cool and reduce stuffiness. Draw nets if you have them across the open windows and doors to keep the bugs out. For best effectiveness do this at the beginning of the day before the house heats up. Think about outside extendible awnings or shutters if this is usually needed every summer. Do all this before thinking about buying fans or air conditioning.

Measure and save

There are various types of energy monitors on the market and you may have been given one by your energy provider. If not, you may be able to borrow them from your council or local library. All you need to do is plug them in to a mains socket in your home and they tell you how much energy your home is consuming in kWs and kW/hrs and possibly in £s too. Don't leave them on the whole time as they do consume a tiny amount of electricity. You can also get battery operated ones, if so use rechargeable batteries. Whichever type you use it makes them quite a useful tool to see how much some things are costing you to run in real time. You can see how much more it is costing you to leave the light on in the hall for example and you can watch your consumption and cost go down before your eyes. It is a good way to show that you are using energy so you can track down those standbys wherever they are hiding.

The gym

It's up to you whether you go to a gym or not. It's not all about getting fit, there's a social side to it too, as well as your own personal physical needs. You could save by not driving to the gym to start with. A treadmill uses up say 700 watts for your warm up and cool down (30 minutes in all), but power walking costs nothing to you or the planet.

Worth bearing in mind if you want to save on membership fees.

What Car?

If buying a new or second hand car, don't forget the running costs. To find out the fuel consumption of your car and the one you want to buy go to the Vehicle Certification

Agency website. See link at the back of the book. If pre 2001 use the vehicle tax band as your guide if no other information is to hand. See link to GOV.UK at back of book.

If you live in a city an electric car might be ideal and will cut your emissions and help local air quality. In the UK there are tax savings and let's not forget petrol savings too, amongst other perks like cheaper/free parking and no congestion charges. There is also a range of other 'greener' car options such as hybrids. In this fast developing sector emissions and overall impact on the environment is reducing, with constantly 'greener' cars coming to the forecourt. Now that all cars are rated in terms of CO_2 emissions it is much easier to choose what is right for you.

However green your car is, use public transport as much as possible or walk for an even cheaper and greener option to further reduce your carbon footprint and of course save you money too.

Water

Principles

✓ Save it

✓ Don't waste it

✓ Think before you put it down the sink

Horrendous Household fact:

'The UK has less rainfall per person than our northern European neighbours, and London is drier than Istanbul! (Waterwise, 2014).

In the UK every person uses approximately 150 litres of water a day, a figure that has been growing every year by 1% since 1930. If you take into account the water that is needed to produce the food and products you consume in your day-to-day life (known as embedded water) you actually consume 3400 litres per day (Waterwise, 2014).

There is plenty of water on the planet; the tricky bit is providing enough safe, clean, drinking water when and where we need it. And of course we can have too much of it too. The water in our taps first has to go through an expensive cleaning process, so that it is safe to drink straight from the tap—no matter if you drink it, cook with it, shower with it or use it to wash the car. It seems a bit at odds that we should clean the car with something that has been purified so much that it is good enough to drink!

Not wasting water does not have to compromise your quality of life. It is as simple as using a water butt winter and summer, inside as well as outside the house, having a basin in your sink and fixing any leaks quickly. This will make a huge difference to reducing your water consumption and subsequent bills, and conserve precious drinking water too.

Water meter

If you don't have a water meter, this is something worth considering, as you will be paying for the amount you are using instead of a fixed rate for your property. Your water supplier should fit a water meter at no charge to you. Ideal if you do not waste water and there are only a few people living in your home.

Contact your local water supplier for advice and installation. See link to OFWAT leaflet at back.

Water consumption

When buying new appliances, remember to ensure they are the most water efficient ones. As well as saving the planet you will be saving on water and energy bills, as the less water you use the less you need to heat. A good example of this is when buying a new shower head.

For more information on this, see the bathroom section.

Grey Water In the kitchen

'Grey' water is water you have used once already. It is not 100% clean but it's still useful. If you use it when you can, this saves using fresh drinking water from the tap. For example, don't pour left over tap water from used drinking glasses down the sink, pour it onto the plants or into the watering can or add to the washing up bowl when rinsing dishes before stacking them into the dishwasher. There are various suggestions throughout the book and perhaps you can think of a few more places too.

Grey water in the garden

You might be able to use some grey water for these jobs too. For cleaning out bins, washing the car, rinsing wellington boots and other things that don't need to be cleaned with fresh drinking water.

Use a water butt

Use a water butt for watering plants inside as well as outside and don't forget to fill vases with water butt water.

No water butt

If you do not have a water butt you can make your own or leave your bucket/wheelbarrow outside, you will be surprised how quickly it fills up. Or adapt your old plastic bin into a water butt.

If you live in a climate where mosquitos are common, please ensure you follow proper guidelines and rules in your area.

You don't need a hose

Use water from the water butt first. When the butt is empty use a bucket and fill from the tap instead of using a hose as you will use less water this way.

No need for sprinkler

Avoid using a sprinkler. Established plants in the garden should not need watering, so only do the sensitive plants and/or the fruit-bearing ones.

Washing outside

If washing down garden furniture or a bike for example, do it outside on the grass (when the sun has gone in the summer) without using detergent. It helps water the grass and surrounding plants at the same time.

Washing the car	Use water from the water butt. If you use it to rinse the soapsuds off you will not need to leather-off as the water butt water will leave no streaks, saving loads of effort and time.	
Plug in!	Always put the plug in first and then turn on the tap. Turn off the tap as soon as you have enough water. For minimal water use ensure the plug is in before you start.	
Turn the tap off	Do not leave the tap running while cleaning your teeth. OFWAT, the government regulator of the water industry in England and Wales states 'A running tap uses up to nine litres of water a minute. *(OFWAT, 2014)* 'A dripping hot water tap wastes energy and in one week wastes enough hot water to fill half a bath...' *(Energy Saving Trust, 2014)*	
Dripping taps	Fix dripping taps without delay, it could save you over £18 a year! *(Waterwise, 2014)*. A good idea is to have a bowl in the sink at all times this way you can spot any leaks and collect any water. A dripping tap can waste more than 5,500 litres of water a year. That's enough to fill a paddling pool every week for the whole summer! *(Waterwise, 2014)*.	

Banish the bath

No need to use the bath, use the shower instead. OFWAT states 'A five-minute shower uses about 40 litres of water. This is about half the volume of a standard bath.' (*OFWAT, 2014*)

'If everybody in your family of four replaces one bath a week with a five minute shower, you can save up to £15 a year on gas bills and up to £25 on water bills (if you have a water meter). (*Energy Saving Trust, 2014*)

Shower

Avoid running the taps or a showerhead while waiting for the hot water for your shower. If you must, at the very least don't turn on the shower until you are in there and hold the shower in your hand away from you. Then turn it on and wait until it is hot enough for you. Every second counts and a minute of wasted water costs you energy and water bills.

Remember to turn the tap off too while shampooing, applying soap, etc. If you don't want to do that, wash your hair separately, bending over the bath/shower tray and turning the water off in between applying shampoo.

'On average a shower uses 10 litres of water a minute.' (*Thames Water, 2014*)

Heads up for showers

Replacing your showerhead with an efficient one could save you around £75 a year off your gas bill for a typical family of 4 and around £90 off your water bill each year. If you have a water meter, that's £165! (*Energy Saving Trust, 2014*)

There are various options on the market, and they can halve your shower water consumption but enhance the shower feel by sucking in air for a gorgeous luxury feel. Of course the less water you use the less energy you use to heat it. Suitable for power showers without reduced performance, but not suitable for electric showers.

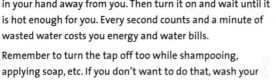
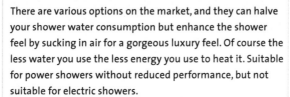

Toilet flushing	You can further reduce the water you use by not flushing every time you go – if it's yellow let it mellow. This can easily be done at night so as not to wake the house, and/or apply to the upstairs toilet only, asking visitors to use the downstairs loo instead. 'On average, each flush uses 7 litres of water.' (*Thames Water, 2014*)	

Water saving labelling	The Waterwise Recommended Checkmark means 'this product is a recognized water saver'. The label sits alongside other labels, such as the Bathroom Manufacturer's Association Label, which uses an A-G classification for the water consumption of products. It is a voluntary product-labelling scheme for water-saving products.	

Collecting water in the kitchen	When rinsing a mug before making another cup of tea or rinsing a plate before stacking in the dishwasher, do it over a bowl in the sink and collect the water. After a while you don't need to turn the tap on to rinse, just use this 'grey' water and then stack in the dishwasher or put to one side to wash up in clean hot water later.	

Doing the dishes	Always ensure you use a bowl or put the plug in before you start. You could reduce water wastage by 50% (*Waterwise, 2014*).	
Washing up	If you don't have a dishwasher, rinsing dirty plates in this way saves work, water and energy. Do the washing up when you have enough or at the end of the day, so you only need to use one bowl full and do it once.	
Washing up bowl in the summer	Spare water collected in the bowl that hasn't had any detergent in it can be used to water plants in the garden around their roots when cool. This saves using your water butt, which will get a lot of use in the summer.	
Dishwasher ... *I write this note for all those mums that try to cook dinner and find they first need some wire wool to clean the pot.*	Stack the dishwasher full before putting it on. If pre rinsed in the sink as above, use a shorter setting, which skips rinsing it again and depending on the machine may use a lower temperature. This saves time, energy, and water and increases the life of your dishwasher. For those new to the wonders of the dishwasher, such as teenagers, burnt on stains will get baked on in the drying cycle if they are not removed in the washing cycle, so I prefer to rinse by hand especially as I do not put the dishwasher on every day. A mistake most of us will notice when empting the dishwasher and one you should only make once, as it is a real pain to clean off requiring serious elbow grease.	

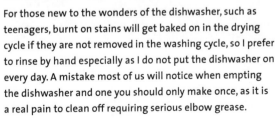

191

| Pets and water | With an empty bowl in the sink rinse out the pet water container and refill with fresh water. The water remaining in the bowl is 'grey' water and can be used elsewhere in the house and garden as highlighted in various places in the book. | |

| Reuse kettle water | Whenever you empty the kettle make it work. Rinse the drainer, poor left over boiling water on weeds in the patio to kill them, use to clean or rinse dirty dishes.

There should never be a need to just tip water down the sink. |  |

| Cleaning fruit and vegetables | When cleaning fruit and veg put the tap over a bowl so you collect the water and turn off the water when you have enough in the bowl. The remaining water can then go and be used to water the plants inside or out or pre-rinse dishes. | |

| Boiling water | Use a kettle and only boil the water you need to save water and energy (Waterwise, 2014). It's quicker too. You can measure out the water you need and then put it in the kettle to boil if you wish. Or you could use your microwave if you wish. | |

Drinking water

UK tap water for drinking is perfectly safe. It is also stringently tested and regulated (*Water UK, 2013*), so for me the safer option.

Saves money and unnecessary carrying too.

Tap is good

When getting water from the tap to drink, do not let the tap run until it gets cold as this wastes perfectly good water too. It can waste more than 10 litres of tap water a day (*Waterwise, 2014*).

Instead, keep a jug of tap water in the fridge so it is ready to use, perfectly chilled, safe and tastes great with no waiting. To ensure the water is always fresh, use it within 24 hours or empty out and fill up a fresh bottle each day (*South West Water, 2013*).

You can empty out onto the plants or use as you would grey water to rinse before stacking the dishwasher etc.

Cooking pots

Use a pot with a lid. It uses less water to cook, and cooks quicker at a lower temperature (*Waterwise, 2014*).

Steam cook

Use a steamer or steamer basket in your pot to use even less water, energy and time. This method of cooking reduces the loss of minerals and vitamins compared to boiling too. *Institute for Optimum Nutrition (1992)*.

| **Washing up** | If washing up by hand clean glasses first and leave the dirtiest till last to make the bubbles and water last longer. |  |

| **Airing clothes** | You don't always need to wash everything after wearing once if you haven't stained the garment, maybe it needs just airing. You can air inside on a hanger in the room (not in the wardrobe) or over the back of chair or outside on the washing line. If it does not smell fresh after two days always put it in the washing basket. When you wash your clothes over time the colours can fade and they lose shape, so you are saving money in clothes buying in the long run too by not washing them unnecessarily. | |

| **Washing machine** | Only wash clothes when you have a full load. Half a load of washing does not mean you will use half the amount of energy or water, so find something else that needs washing or wait till you have enough. | |

| **Split it into two washes only** | If that means you don't spin to save doing a separate wash that's what you do. Wash dark colours (socks, jeans, briefs, dark t-shirts, kitchen cloths, sponges) at 30°C– no spin is required – then line dry. Lights: (work/school shirts, t-shirts, light underwear, towels and bedding). Depending on the mix, wash at 30°C or 40°C with or without spin. When you have no bedding or towels you can rub on a stain remover on collars and cuffs and put in at 30°C before opting for a hotter wash and increased energy bills. | |

Hand wash and soaking

Save up a few items so you can reuse the water by doing all the light colours first. It will reduce water and energy used as well as time.

Cleaning your teeth

This is a job done at least 2 to 3 times a day where you can cut down the water used each time, which all adds up. Put the plug in first. Turn the tap off while brushing your teeth as a running tap uses an incredible 6 litres plus a minute, so turning the tap off could save you around 12–18 litres each time! (*Waterwise, 2014*). All you need to do is turn the tap on to wet the toothbrush. There's no need to keep the water running. Drain and rinse the sink afterwards.

Water hippo

On average we use around 30% of all the clean, drinkable water in our homes to flush! (*Waterwise, 2014*).

A water hippo or similar (1 litre tub or bag) reduces water used for each flush by 1 litre. Over the year that could add up to 5,000 litres of water (*Waterwise, 2014*). You can buy one or make your own by using an old ice cream tub. Put something in it like a large pebble to make sure it stays at the bottom of the cistern. Put the lid on so no water can get in and then submerge in the toilet cistern, where it will not interfere with the flushing lever. You want to be able to flush and allow the lever to come back so it does not constantly flush. It does not require any DIY skills but if not sure how to do it, seek advice first. Not suitable for toilets that have a cistern below 6 litres.

You could save between one and three litres each time you flush the toilet with a water saving device. (*OFWAT, 2014*)

Your local water company might provide you a save-a-flush bag for free, so visit their website to find out what is on offer.

Toilet or watery grave

If you use the toilet to get rid of things like hair off your brush, or toilet paper with hair removal cream and other such odd bits and pieces that are destined for a watery grave, don't waste water flushing it down. Just leave in bowl and flush the next time you go.

New toilet?

If you need to buy a new toilet, make sure you are getting a water efficient one with a dual flush to save water, which remember you are paying for.

Dual split-flush toilets typically use 4-6 litres of water; if you have an old style one they could use 13 litres per flush. (*Waterwise, 2014*).

Shower or bath

A shower uses less water than a bath, so banish the bath.

OFWAT states 'A five-minute shower uses about 40 litres of water. This is about half the volume of a standard bath.' (*OFWAT, 2014*)

Remember to turn the water off too while shampooing, applying soap, especially if you have a power shower. This saves water and heating costs. If you don't want to do that you could wash your hair separately leaning into the shower or bath.

Of course sharing a bath or shower saves even more water and energy ...*what fun!*

'If everybody in your family of four replaces one bath a week with a five minute shower, you can save up to £15 a year on gas bills and up to £25 on water bills (if you have a water meter), (*Energy Saving Trust, 2015*).

Showerheads

Replacing your showerhead with an efficient one is 'an easy way to save both water and energy'. *(Energy Saving Trust, 2015)*. You could save you around £75 a year off your gas bill for a typical family of 4 and around £90 off your water bill each year. If you have a water meter, that's £165!

There are various options on the market and they can halve your shower water consumption but enhance the shower feel by sucking in air for a gorgeous super-soft luxury feel. Of course the less water you use the less energy you use to heat it. Suitable for power showers without reduced performance, but not suitable for electric showers.

Water saving devices

When replacing showerheads, taps, washing machines etc. Look for water efficient versions.

Taps

How much water you use every time you turn the tap on can vary hugely from 2-25 litres per minute *(Waterwise, 2014)*.

The quick and simple solution is to fit an aerator tap insert, which only costs a couple of pounds into your tap. As well as saving water every time you turn on the tap you are also saving energy each time you use the hot tap too!

When buying new fittings make sure it has an aerator and/or is a low water consumption tap.

Toilet flushing

You can further reduce the water you use by not flushing every time you go. For the truly committed I would say if it's yellow let it mellow. This can easily be done at night, not to wake the house. If you have a downstairs toilet, have a ready for visitors' policy and instead leave clean and go upstairs to the loo.

Writing this book...

... started out as a bit of a hobby while I was living in Paris. There, time was on my side and the inspiration of all that sightseeing fuelled a desire to put down all the things floating around in my head on paper. My basic goal was simple enough, to help and inspire us to do the right everyday things for the planet and show us all it does not have to compromise our quality of life. Hopefully I have shown what can be done and focused on the benefits for us directly, as well as the benefits to our environment.

It seems over the years this hobby has now become a bit of a passion. I see this book as the beginning of what we can all do, and not the definitive end. The future is all about progress and change, not stagnation.

Innovation and need will create greater opportunities for us all to do the right thing more. I hope you have enjoyed this little book and found it useful, I too have learnt a lot through this compelling journey.

At the beginning, it all started with me wanting to pass down what I thought was my instinctive sense of what to do in varying scenarios dealt to me at birth by my genes and heightened by my experience in the environmental sector. But I think equally it was down to what my mother so subtly taught me through those formative years, without my even noticing. Therefore I want to say a special thank you to mum and best friend. As all best friends do I have chosen a nice picture below of mum in the 60s.

My Mum in the 1960s

199

Reference List

Act on Energy (2013) Energy Consumption [Internet].
Available at: http://www.actonenergy.org.uk/energy-consumption [Accessed 2 April 2014].

Affordable Warmth Network (2013) Easy save Leaflet

Allergy UK (2013) Chemical sensitivity [Internet].
Available at: http://www.allergyuk.org/chemical-sensitivity/handy-hints-for-chemical-sensitivity [Accessed 5 March 2014].

American Lung Association (2013) Bacteria and viruses [Internet].
Available at: http://www.lung.org/healthy-air/home/resources/bacteria-and-viruses.html [Accessed 31 January 2014].

American Lung Association (2013) Cleaning supplies and household chemicals [Internet].
Available at: http://www.lung.org/healthy-air/home/resources/cleaning-supplies.html [Accessed 31 January 2014].

Anglian Water Services (2013) Hartlepool Water [Internet].
Available at: http://www.hartlepoolwater.co.uk/household/healthy-black-mould.aspx [Accessed 4 February 2014].

Association of Manufacturers of Domestic Appliances (2014) Microwaves [Internet].
Available at: http://www.t2c.org.uk/cooking/microwaves/ [Accessed 7 May 2014].

Asthma UK (2013) Healthy indoor environments [Internet].
Available at: http://www.asthma.org.uk/about-asthma/living-with-asthma/healthy-indoor-environments/ [Accessed 5 March 2014].

Automobile Association (2013) Eco-driving advice [Internet].
Available at: http://www.theaa.com/motoring_advice/fuels-and-environment/drive-smart.html [Accessed 16 January 2014].

BBC (2013) Gardening basics [Internet].
Available at: http://www.bbc.co.uk/gardening/basics/techniques/ [Accessed 1 April 2014].

BBC (2013) Gardening guides [Internet].
Available at: http://www.bbc.co.uk/gardening/basics/techniques/organic_lawn1.shtml [Accessed 1 April 2014].

BBC Science (2013) Healthy eating [Internet].
Available at: http://www.bbc.co.uk/science/0/22028519 [Accessed 22 January 2014].

Beena's Beauty Clinic, Buckinghamshire (2013)

The British Beekeepers Association (2013) Importance of Bees [Internet].
Available at: http://www.bbka.org.uk/kids/importance_of_bees [Accessed 1 January 2015].

BigOven (2013) [Internet].
Available at: http://www.bigoven.com [Accessed 22 January 2014].

British Gas (2013) Laundry tips [Internet].
Available at: http://www.britishgas.co.uk/smarter-living/save-energy/energy-saving-tips.html [Accessed 27 February 2014].

blacktoxicmolds.com (2014) Does vinegar kill mold [Internet].
Available at: http://blacktoxicmolds.com/vinegar-kill-mold.php [Accessed 5 March 2014].

BUPA UK (2013) Atopic eczema symptoms [Internet].
Available at: http://www.bupa.co.uk/individuals/health-information/directory/e/eczema [Accessed 5 March 2014].

BUPA UK (2013) Hydration for exercise – sports drinks [Internet].
Available at: http://www.bupa.co.uk/individuals/health-information/health-news-index/2013/160413-keeping-topped-up-for-exercise-sports-drinks [Accessed 20 January 2014].

Carbon Trust (2014) How to implement thermostatic radiator valves [Internet].
Available at: https://www.carbontrust.com/media/147135/j7961_ctl040_thermostatic_radiator_valves_aw.pdf [Accessed 3 April 2014].

Chelsea and Westminster Hospital (2013) Dermatology skin care [Internet].
Available at:*http://www.chelwest.nhs.uk/your-visit/leaflets/med/Dermatology-Skin-Care.pdf/view* [Accessed 3 April 2014].

Channel4 (2014) Embarrassing Bodies [Internet].
Available at: *http://www.channel4embarrassingillnesses.com/men-in-white-coats/itching/treatment/* [Accessed 12 February 2014].

The Childrens Oral Health Institute (2014) Project clean toothbrush [Internet].
Available at: *http://www.mycohi.org* [Accessed 7 February 2014].

Colgate-Palmolive (UK) Limited (2013) Q&A [Internet].
Available at: *http://www.colgate.co.uk/app/ColgateOralCare/ElectricToothbrush/ProClinical/UK/EN/QandA.cwsp* [Accessed 11 February 2014].

California Energy Commission (2014) Consumer energy centre, refrigerators and freezers [Internet].
Available at: *http://www.consumerenergycenter.org/residential/appliances/refrigerators.html* [Accessed 7 May 2014].

Charities Aid Foundation (2015) 2014 Publications [Internet] Available at: *https://www.cafonline.org/about-us/publications/2014-publications/world-giving-index-2014* [Accessed 6 September 2015].

Dri-Pak Ltd (2014) Bicarbonate of Soda, cleaning, deodorising [Internet].
Available at *http://www.dri-pak.co.uk/bicarbonate-of-soda.html#.UuaH2Po4lXQ* [Accessed 27 January 2014].

Dri-Pak Ltd (2014) Cleaning tips for the kitchen [Internet].
Available at: *http://www.dri-pak.co.uk/kitchen-cleaning-tips/dishwashers.html#.UukuCfo4lXQ* [Accessed 29 January 2014].

Dr. Oetker (2014) What else can I use baking soda for [Internet].
Available at: *http://www.oetker.co.uk/oetker_uk/frequently_asked_questions/baking_faqs/what_else_can_i_use_bicarbonate_of_soda_for.html* [Accessed 5 March 2014].

Dryerballs Ltd (2012) Where to buy [Internet].
Available at: *http://www.dryerballs.co.uk/enviroment.html* [Accessed 27 February 2014].

EcoZone Limited (2013) Ecoballs 240 [Internet].
Available at: *http://www.ecozone.com/products/ecoballs_240* [Accessed 19 February 2014].

EcoZone Limited (2013) Ecoballs 240 instructions leaflet.

Edinburgh Community Food (2013) Fruit and vegetables [Internet].
Available at: *http://www.edinburghcommunityfood.org.uk/assets/files/documents/WhatToStore.pdf* [Accessed 20 January 2014].

eHow (2013) Cheap ways to make your house smell good [Internet].
Available at: *http://www.ehow.com/info_8262281_cheap-make-house-smell-good.html* [Accessed 21 March 2014].

eHow (2013) How to clean with carbonated water [Internet].
Available at: *http://www.ehow.com/how_5888349_clean-carbonated-water.html* [Accessed 27 February 2014].

eHow (2013) What is the difference between unrefined & refined can sugar? [Internet].
Available at: *http://www.ehow.co.uk/facts_5968825_difference-unrefined-refined-cane-sugar_.html* [Accessed 2 April 2014].

Encyclopaedia Britannica, Noelle Eckley Selin (2013) Carbon Footprint [Internet].
Available at: *http://www.britannica.com/EBchecked/topic/1585219/carbon-footprint* [Accessed 22 January 2014].

Energy Saving Trust (2015) Energy efficient lighting [Internet].
Available at: *http://www.energysavingtrust.org.uk/domestic/content/energy-efficient-lighting* [Accessed 25 January 2015].

Energy Saving Trust (2015) Energy saving light bulbs [Internet].
Available at: *http://www.energysavingtrust.org.uk/domestic/content/energy-saving-light-bulbs* [Accessed 25 January 2015].

Energy Saving Trust (2013) Insulation [Internet].
Available at: *http://www.energysavingtrust.org.uk/Insulation/Insulating-tanks-pipes-and-radiators* [Accessed 3 April 2014].

Energy Saving Trust (2013) Insulation, cavity wall insulation [Internet].
Available at: *http://www.energysavingtrust.org.uk/Insulation/Cavity-wall-insulation* [Accessed 3 April 2014].

Energy Saving Trust (2013) Insulation, Roof and Loft [Internet].
Available at: *http://www.energysavingtrust.org.uk/Insulation/Roof-and-loft-insulation* [Accessed 3 April 2014].

Energy Saving Trust (2013) Insulation, Solid wall insulation [Internet].
Available at: *http://www.energysavingtrust.org.uk/Insulation/Solid-wall-insulation* [Accessed 3 April 2014].

Energy Saving Trust (2013) Insulation, Wall insulation [Internet].
Available at: http://www.energysavingtrust.org.uk/Insulation/Wall-insulation [Accessed 3 April 2014].

Energy Saving Trust (2013) Products and Appliances [Internet].
Available at: *http://www.energysavingtrust.org.uk/Electricity/Products-and-appliances#kitchen* [Accessed 23 January 2014].

Energy Saving Trust (2013) Saving money on water heating [Internet].
Available at: *http://www.energysavingtrust.org.uk/Heating-and-hot-water/Saving-money-on-water* [Accessed 3 April 2014].

Energy Saving Trust (2005) Save your 20%, Booklet, p.2

Energy Saving Trust (2013) Take-action [Internet].
Available at: *http://www.energysavingtrust.org.uk/Take-action/Energy-saving-top-tips* [Accessed 23 January 2014].

Energy Saving Trust (2013) Trouble in the pipeline [Internet].
Available at: *http://www.energysavingtrust.org.uk/blog/2012/02/17/trouble-in-the-pipeline/* [Accessed 27 January 2014].

Energy Saving Trust (2014) Thermostats and controls [Internet].
Available at: *http://www.energysavingtrust.org.uk/Heating-and-hot-water/Thermostats-and-controls* [Accessed 3 April 2014].

Energy Saving Trust (2014) Vast scale of Britain's water use revealed [Internet].
Available at: *http://www.energysavingtrust.org.uk/Energy-Saving-Trust/Press/Press-releases/Vast-scale-of-Britain-s-water-use-revealed-in-new-report* [Accessed 7 May 2014].

Energy Saving Trust (2015) Saving water [Internet].
Available at: *http://www.energysavingtrust.org.uk/domestic/content/saving-water* [Accessed 26 January 2015].

Energy Saving Trust (2015) Energy efficient windows [Internet].
Available at: *http://www.energysavingtrust.org.uk/domestic/content/energy-efficient-windows* [Accessed 26 January 2015].

Energy Saving Trust (2015) Home appliances [Internet].
Available at: *http://www.energysavingtrust.org.uk/domestic/content/home-appliances* [Accessed 25 January 2015].

Enterprise Utilities (2015) Energy efficient boilers [Internet].
Available at: *http://energyeu.co.uk/energy-efficient-boilers/ [Accessed 25 January 2015].*

Environmental Protection Agency (2013) Climate Change [Internet].
Available at: *http://www.epa.gov/climatechange/basics/* [Accessed 14 January 2014].

Environmental Protection Agency (2014) Overview of greenhouse gases [Internet].
Available at: *http://epa.gov/climatechange/ghgemissions/gases/ch4.html* [Accessed 4 June 2014].

Environmental Protection Agency (2015) Batteries Common Wastes & Materials [Internet].
Available at: *http://www.epa.gov/osw/conserve/materials/battery.htm [Accessed 1 February 2015].*

Environix (2014) Odour Removal [Internet].
Available at: *http://www.environix.co.uk/odour-removal.html* [Accessed 14 5 March 2014].

EnviroProducts Ltd (2013) E-Cloth [Internet].
Available at: *http://www.e-cloth.com* [Accessed 27 January 2014].

EnviroProducts Ltd (2013) Get the most out of your e-cloth [Internet].
Available at: *http://www.e-cloth.com/pages/usecare* [Accessed 27 February 2014].

E.On UK plc (2013) 99 Energy saving tips [Internet].
Available at: *http://www.eon-uk.com/media/511.aspx* [Accessed 28 March 2014].

Food Standards Agency (2012) Food safety Week 2012 [Internet].
Available at: *http://www.food.gov.uk/news-updates/campaigns/germwatch/#.URoaKaXonzl* [Accessed 20 January 2014].

Food Standards Agency (2012) How chilled is your fridge? [Internet].
Available at: *http://www.food.gov.uk/northern-ireland/nutritionni/niyoungpeople/survivorform/dontgetsick/chilling*
[Accessed 26 January 2015]

Forest Stewardship Council (2013) Frequently asked questions [Internet].
Available at: *http://www.fsc-uk.org/frequently-asked-questions.31.htm* [Accessed 1 April 2014].

The Freecycle Network (2013) [Internet].
Available at: *http://www.freecycle.org* [Accessed 17 January 2014].

Futerra Sustainability Communications Ltd (2014) Swishing [Internet].
Available at: *http://swishing.com/home/* [Accessed 17 January 2014].

Fyffes (2013) Storage and Care [Internet].
Available at: *http://www.fyffes.com/gns/our-fruit/fyffes-bananas/Storage-and-care.aspx* [Accessed 20 January 2014].

Glass & Glazing Federation (2014) Publications [Internet].
Available at: *http://www.ggf.org.uk/publication/replacement_windows_and_doors_environmental_checklist*
[Accessed 3 June 2014].

Guildford Cleaning Company (2014) Oven cleaning using bicarbonate of soda [Internet].
Available at: *http://www.guildfordcleaningcompany.co.uk/blog/oven-cleaning-using-bicarbonate-of-soda*
[Accessed 28 January 2014]

H.C. Plumbing & Gas Services (2013) Boilers and central heating systems [Internet].
Available at: *http://www.hcplumbing.co.uk/combi%20boilers%20central%20heating.htm* [Accessed 3 April 2014].

Homeguides (2013) Natural brass copper cleaner [Internet].
Available at: *http://homeguides.sfgate.com/natural-brass-copper-cleaner-78688.html* [Accessed 5 March 2014].

Honour Your Flow (2014) [Internet].
Available at: *http://www.honouryourflow.co.uk* [Accessed 28 January 2014].

How stuff Works (2014) How drain cleaners work [Internet].
Available at: *http://home.howstuffworks.com/home-improvement/plumbing/drain-cleaner3.htm* [Accessed 4 February 2014].

Incpen (2006) 3rd ed. Reading:

Institute for Optimum Nutrition (1992) [Internet].
Available at: *http://www.ion.ac.uk/information/onarchives/whatscooking* [Accessed 23 January 2014].

John Lewis department stores (2013) leaflet on Waste electrical, electronic equipment (WEEE) and recycling batteries reference SD74598/ 03.10

Julesave Limited (2014) Heatkeeper energy saving radiator panels [Internet].
Available at: *http://www.heatkeeper.co.uk/energy-saving-and-other-benefits.html* [Accessed 3 April 2014].

Local Farmers Markets (2007) Find a Farmers Market [Internet].
Available at: *http://www.local-farmers-markets.co.uk/find-farmers-market.html* [Accessed 16 January 2014].

Love British Food (2013) What's in season when [Internet].
Available at: *http://www.lovebritishfood.co.uk/teacher-zone/teacher-zone/whats-in-season-when/* [Accessed 17 January 2014].

Med-Health (2014) Avocado oil for skin [Internet].
Available at: *http://www.med-health.net/Avocado-Oil-For-Skin.html* [Accessed 29 January 2014].

Mistral Lab Supplies (2014) Sodium carbonate decahydrate [Internet].
Available at: *http://mistralni.co.uk/products/soda-crystals-washing-soda* [Accessed 29 January 2014].

**National Geographic (2013) Quiz [Internet]. Available at: <http://environment.nationalgeographic.com/environment/
energy/great-energy-challenge/food-water-energy-quiz/> [Accessed 14 January 2014].**

National Geographic (2013) Quiz [Internet].
Available at: *http://environment.nationalgeographic.com/environment/energy/great-energy-challenge/food-water-energy-quiz/* [Accessed 14 January 2014].

National Geographic (2013) Quiz [Internet].
Available at: *http://environment.nationalgeographic.com/environment/energy/great-energy-challenge/food-water-energy-quiz/* [Accessed 14 January 2014].

National Geographic (2013) Quiz [Internet].
Available at: *http://environment.nationalgeographic.com/environment/energy/great-energy-challenge/food-water-energy-quiz/* [Accessed 14 January 2014].

National Geographic (2013) Quiz [Internet].
Available at: *http://environment.nationalgeographic.com/environment/energy/great-energy-challenge/food-water-energy-quiz/* [Accessed 14 January 2014].

Net Doctor (2013) What's the best way of cleaning ears [Internet].
Available at: *http://www.netdoctor.co.uk/ate/ent/202825.html* [Accessed 13 February 2014].

NHS (2013) How to you're your teeth clean [Internet].
Available at: *http://www.nhs.uk/Livewell/dentalhealth/Pages/Teethcleaningguide.aspx* [Accessed 7 February 2014].

NHS (2013) The eatwell plate [Internet].
Available at: *http://www.nhs.uk/Livewell/Goodfood/Pages/eatwell-plate.aspx* [Accessed 22 January 2014].

NHS (2013) How to store food safely [Internet].
Available at: *http://www.nhs.uk/Livewell/homehygiene/Pages/how-to-store-food-safely.aspx* [Accessed 23 January 2014].

NHS (2014) Child health information factsheet – House dust mites [Internet].
Available at: *http://www.uhs.nhs.uk/Media/Controlleddocuments/Patientinformation/Childhealth/Housedustmite-patientinformation.pdf* [Accessed 4 June 2014].

NHS (2013) Home Hygiene [Internet].
Available at: *http://www.nhs.uk/Livewell/homehygiene/Pages/Foodpoisoningtips.aspx* [Accessed 27 January 2014].

NHS (2013) Vitamins and minerals [Internet].
Available at: *http://www.nhs.uk/conditions/vitamins-minerals/Pages/vitamins-minerals.aspx* [Accessed 20 January 2014].

NHS (2013) Can reheating rice cause food poisoning? [Internet].
Available at: *http://www.nhs.uk/chq/Pages/can-reheating-rice-cause-food-poisoning.aspx?CategoryID=51* [Accessed 20 January 2014].

NHS (2013) What should my daily intake of calories be? [Internet].
Available at: *http://www.nhs.uk/chq/Pages/1126.aspx?CategoryID=51&SubCategoryID=164* [Accessed 22 January 2014].

NHS (2014) Self treatment of common illnesses and accidents [Internet].
Available at: *http://www.nhs.uk/services/gp/overview/defaultview.aspx?id=42797* [Accessed 7 February 2014].

nutrition.about.com (2013) What nutrients are lost when fruits and Vegetables are Cut? [Internet].
Available at: *http://nutrition.about.com/od/askyournutritionist/f/cutveg.htm* [Accessed 16 January 2014].

OFWAT (2014) Water saving tips [Internet].
Available at: *http://www.ofwat.gov.uk/consumerissues/conservingwater/tips/* [Accessed 30 January 2014].

Dr Peterson, D. (2014) Mouth Rinses [Internet].
Available at: *http://www.dentalgentlecare.com/mouthrinses.htm* [Accessed 7 February 2014].

Premium Light (2014) Quality and efficiency [Internet].
Available at: *http://www.premiumlight.eu/index.php?page=step-2-quality-and-efficiency-criteria-6* [Accessed 31 March 2014].

Raymond Blanc (2014) Tips [Internet].
Available at: *http://www.brasserieblanc.com/raymond-blanc/tips.php* [Accessed 16 January 2014].

Readers Digest (2013) 9 Extraordinary use for bananas [Internet].
Available at: *http://www.rd.com/home/9-extraordinary-uses-for-bananas/* [Accessed 23 January 2014].

Readers Digest (2013) 7 Extraordinary uses for olive oil [Internet].
Available at: *http://www.rd.com/slideshows/7-extraordinary-uses-for-olive-oil/#slideshow=slide6* [Accessed 19 March 2014].

Readers Digest (2014) 10 tips for healthy, white teeth [Internet].
Available at: *http://www.rd.com/slideshows/10-tips-for-healthy-whiter-teeth/#slideshow=slide6* [Accessed 7 February 2014].

Readers Digest (2014) How to get rid of body odour [Internet].
Available at: *http://www.readersdigest.co.uk/health/embarrassing-conditions/body-odour/how-get-rid-body-odour* [Accessed 12 February 2014].

Readers Digest (2013) How to wash shower curtains [Internet].
Available at: *http://www.rd.com/home/how-to-wash-shower-curtains/* [Accessed 27 February 2014].

The Royal Borough of Kensington and Chelsea (2013) Indoor Air Quality [Internet].
Available at: *http://www.rbkc.gov.uk/environmentandtransport/airquality/indoorairquality.aspx* [Accessed 27 January 2014].

Saltworks (2014) Salt uses and tips [Internet].
Available at: *http://www.saltworks.us/salt_info/salt-uses-and-tips.asp* [Accessed 26 January 2014].

Salveo (2013) Soap nuts [Internet].
Available at: *http://www.salveo.co.uk/soap-nuts-natural-laundry-detergent-from-salveo-1kg-bag.html* [Accessed 26 February 2014].

Science Daily (2008) Eating Less Meat And Junk Food Could Cut Fossil Energy Fuel Use Almost In Half [Internet].
Available at: *http://www.sciencedaily.com/releases/2008/07/080723094838.htm* [Accessed 22 January 2014].

The Soap Kitchen (2014) Bicarbonate of soda [Internet].
Available at: *http://www.thesoapkitchen.co.uk/bicarb_of_soda.htm* [Accessed 5 March 2014].

South West Water (2013) Drinking water quality [Internet].
Available at: *http://www.southwestwater.co.uk/index.cfm?articleid=11230* [Accessed 22 January 2014].

Storingandfreezing.co.uk (2013) How to Freeze Dairy Products [Internet].
Available at: *http://www.storingandfreezing.co.uk/how-freeze-dairy-products.html* [Accessed 22 January 2014].

Thames Water (2014) Waterwisely [Internet].
Available at: *http://secure.thameswater.co.uk/waterwisely/index.htm#!/tips.htm* [Accessed 30 January 2014].

Thames Water (2013) Water saving tips for gardeners [Internet].
Available at: *http://secure.thameswater.co.uk/waterwisely/index.htm#!/gardening.htm* [Accessed 1 April 2014].

theguardian.com (3 September 2013) Guardian sustainable business [Internet].
Available at: *http://www.theguardian.com/sustainable-business/misshapen-fruit-vegetables-business-case* [Accessed 4 June 2014].

Uswitch.com (2014) Energy-efficient cooking [Internet].
Available at: *http://www.uswitch.com/energy-saving/guides/energy-efficient-cooking/* [Accessed 7 May 2014].

Uswitch.com (2015) Make your laundry more energy-efficient and reduce your energy bills [Internet].
Available at: *http://www.uswitch.com/energy-saving/guides/energy-efficient-laundry/* [Accessed 25 January 2015].

Vacuvin (2013) [Internet].
Available at: *http://www.vacuvin.com/270/Vacuum_Wine_Saver.html* [Accessed 22 January 2014].

Water UK (2013) Looking after water in your home [Internet].
Available: *http://www.water.org.uk/Looking_after_water_in_your_home* [Accessed 23 January 2014].

Waterwise (2013) Fun Facts [Internet].
Available at:*http://www.waterwise.org.uk/pages/fun-facts.html* [Accessed 14 January 2014].

Waterwise (2013) Water The Facts [Internet].
Available at: *http://www.waterwise.org.uk/data/resources/25/Water_factsheet_2012.pdf* [Accessed 15 January 2014].

Waterwise (2014) Reducing water Waste Wastage in the UK [Internet].
Available at: *http://www.waterwise.org.uk/newsletter_archive/reducing_water_wastage_in_the_uk/media_centre/media_kit.html* [Accessed 3 June 2014].

Waterwise (2013) Indoors, Clothes washing [Internet].
Available at: *http://www.waterwise.org.uk/pages/indoors.html#5-* [Accessed 14 January 2014].

Waterwise (2013) Outdoors [Internet].
Available at: *http://www.waterwise.org.uk/pages/outdoors.html* [Accessed 15 January 2014].

Waterwise (2014) Water saving advice and tips [Internet].
Available at: *http://www.waterwise.org.uk/pages/water-saving-advice-and-tips.html#Kitchen* [Accessed 3 June 2014].

Web MD (2013) How to keep your veggies vitamin packed [Internet].
Available at: *http://www.webmd.com/food-recipes/features/how-to-keep-your-veggies-vitamin-packed* [Accessed 16 January 2014].

Web MD (2013) With Fruits and Veggies, More Matters [Internet].
Available at: *http://www.webmd.com/food-recipes/features/fruits-veggies-more-matters* [Accessed 16 January 2014].

What Allergy? (2014) Fighting cold sores [Internet].
Available at: *http://whatallergy.com/2011-02/fighting-cold-sores* [Accessed 7 February 2014].

Which? (2015) FAQs: batteries and battery chargers [Internet].
Available at: *http://www.which.co.uk/home-and-garden/heating-water-and-electricity/reviews-ns/batteries/faqs-batteries-and-battery-chargers/* [Accessed 1 February 2015].

Which? (2014) Energy-efficient fridge freezers [Internet].
Available at:*http://www.which.co.uk/energy/energy-saving-products/reviews-ns/energy-saving-appliances/energy-efficient-fridge-freezers/* [Accessed 23 January 2014].

Which? (2014) How to clean a microwave oven [Internet].
Available at: *http://local.which.co.uk/advice/how-to-clean-microwave* [Accessed 29 January 2014].

Which? (2015) Washing machine temperature guide [Internet].
Available at: *http://www.which.co.uk/reviews/washing-machines/article/advice/washing-machine-temperature-guide* [Accessed 25 January 2015]

WikiHow (2013) How to make your cell phone battery last longer [Internet].
Available at: *http://www.wikihow.com/Make-Your-Cell-Phone-Battery-Last-Longer* [Accessed 1 April 2014].

Wikipedia (2015) *William of Occam quote* [Internet].
Available at: *http://en.wikipedia.org/wiki/Occam's_razor (Thorburn, 1918, pp. 352–3; Kneale and Kneale, 1962, p. 243.)*

Women's Environmental Network (2004) Seeing red sanitary protection and the environment [Internet].
Available at: *http://www.wen.org.uk/wp-content/uploads/sanpro.pdf* [Accessed 13 February 2014].

The World Bank (2012) United Kingdom [Internet].
Available at: *http://www.worldbank.org/en/country/unitedkingdom* [Accessed 16 January 2014].

Worldometers (2013) World Population Clock [Internet].
Available at: *http://www.worldometers.info/world-population/* [Accessed 16 January 2014].

WRAP (Waste & Resources Action Programme) (2013) Love Food Hate Waste [Internet].
Available at: *http://england.lovefoodhatewaste.com/content/great-progress-...-we've-got-long-way-go* [Accessed 14 January 2014].

WRAP (Waste & Resources Action Programme) (2013) Love Food Hate Waste, Best before & use By Date [Internet].
Available at: <*http://england.lovefoodhatewaste.com/node/2285*> [Accessed 20 January 2014].

WRAP (Waste & Resources Action Programme) *Love Food Hate Waste, A Third of the food we buy in the UK end up being thrown away* [Read 20 March 2015].

WRAP (Waste & Resources Action Programme) Facts and figures [Internet]. Available at: *http://www.wrap.org.uk/content/facts-and-figures* [Accessed 5 September 2015].

Bibliography

Alzheimer's Society (2015) Donate old Jewellery [Internet].
Available at: <*http://www.alzheimers.org.uk/site/scripts/documents_info.
php?documentID=532&gclid=CjwKEAjwr6ipBRCM7oqrj6O3ojUSJACff2WHiICojA9NJhkqoB9KrLmnKF_
ihToQcGQwmUCsCbKoWhoC4vbw_wcB*> [Accessed 12 April 2015].

ASOS.com Ltd (2013) Marketplace [Internet].
Available at: *https://marketplace.asos.com/community/thepeoplesrunway?WT.ac=Mktp_Foot_Runway*
[Accessed 26 March 2014].

Beena's Beauty Clinic (2013), http://bbc82.com

The British Beekeepers Association (2013) Gardening for bees [Internet].
Available at: *http://www.bbka.org.uk/learn/gardening_for_bees* [Accessed 1 April 2014].

Community Repaint (2013) [Internet].
Available at: *http://www.communityrepaint.org.uk* [Accessed 2 April 2014].

Country Life Magazine (2013) Raising your own chickens [Internet].
Available at: *http://www.countrylife.co.uk/countryside/article/175074/Raising-your-own-chickens.html* [Accessed 2 April 2014].

The Curtain Exchange (2013) [Internet].
Available at: *thecurtainexchange.net* [Accessed 26 March 2014].

Do-it (2013) Want to volunteer [Internet].
Available at: *http://www.do-it.org.uk* [Accessed 2 April 2014].

Ecoverdirect.com (2014) [Internet].
Available at: *http://www.ecover.com/GB/EN/index.aspx* [Accessed 27 February 2014].

Ecoverdirect.com (2014) Laundry bleach [Internet].
Available at: *http://www.ecoverdirect.com/products/laundry-bleach/elaundbleach400g.aspx?productid=elaundbleach400g....*
[Accessed 27 February 2014].

Energy Saving Trust (2013) Home energy check [Internet].
Available at: *http://hec.est.org.uk* [Accessed 3 April 2014]

ESpares Ltd (2013) [Internet].
Available at: *http://www.espares.co.uk* [Accessed 26 March 2014].

Fairtrade Foundation (2011) [Internet].
Available at: *http://www.fairtrade.org.uk* [Accessed 2 April 2014].

Fashion-conscience.com (2014) [Internet].
Available at: *http://www.fashion-conscience.com* [Accessed 6 June 2014].

The Freecycle Network (2013) [Internet].
Available at: *http://www.freecycle.org* [Accessed 2 April 2014].

Freedom Food (2014) [Internet].
Available at: *http://www.freedomfood.co.uk/aboutus* [Accessed 2 April 2014].

GOV.UK (2014) Vehicle tax rate tables [Internet].
Available at: *https://www.gov.uk/vehicle-tax-rate-tables* [Accessed 3 June 2014].

Great Green Systems (2014) Green Cone [Internet].
Available at: *http://www.greatgreensystems.com/green-cone* [Accessed 2 April 2014].

GreenPan - suppliers of green non-stick frying pans [Internet].
Available at: *http://www.green-pan.co.uk/uk/kyoto-collection-724.htm*

Heap Media (2013) How is Blackle saving energy? [Internet].
Available at: *http://blackle.com/about/* [Accessed 1 April 2014].

Landshare (2013) [Internet].
Available at: *http://www.landshare.net/index/* [Accessed 1 April 2014].

Mailing Preference service (2013) Registration [Internet].
Available at: *www.mpsonline.org.uk/mpsr/mps_choosetype.html* [Accessed 1 April 2014].

Marks & Spencer plc (2013) Recycle your M&S clothes at Oxfam [Internet].
Available at: *http://plana.marksandspencer.com/about/partnerships/oxfam* [Accessed 26 March 2014].

OFWAT (2014) Water meters – your questions answered [Internet].
Available at: *http://www.ofwat.gov.uk/mediacentre/leaflets/prs_lft_101117meters.pdf* [Accessed 3 June 2014].

Pinterest (2014) [Internet].
Available at: *http://www.pinterest.com* [Accessed 26 January 2015]

Screwfix (2013) Timers and controllers [Internet].
Available at: *http://www.screwfix.com/c/electrical-lighting/timers-controllers/cat830128?_dyncharset=UTF-8&_dynSessConf=-1615592800675690894&sortBy=price* [Accessed 1 April 2014]

Swishing Limited (2013) [Internet].
Available at: *http://www.swishing.co.uk* [Accessed 26 March 2014].

Valpak Ltd (2013) Bank locator [Internet].
Available at: *http://www.recycle-more.co.uk/banklocator/banklocator.aspx* [Accessed 1 April 2014].

Vehicle Certification Agency (2013) Car fuel data [Internet].
Available at: *http://carfueldata.direct.gov.uk/search-new-or-used-cars.aspx* [Accessed 3 June 2014].

Vision Aid Overseas (2013) [Internet].
Available at: *http://www.visionaidoverseas.org* [Accessed 1 April 2014]

Wikipedia (2013) [Internet].
Available at: *http://en.wikipedia.org/wiki/Food_miles* [Accessed 1 April 2014]

Wiggly Wigglers (2013) Wormery update [Internet].
Available at: *http://www.wigglywigglers.co.uk/wormery-update* [Accessed 2 April 2014]

Which? (2014) Fridge freezers lifetime energy costs tool [Internet].
Available at: *http://www.which.co.uk/home-and-garden/kitchen/guides/fridge-freezer-energy-costs/* [Accessed 7 May 2014]

Which? (2014) Dishwasher energy costs [Internet].
Available at: *http://www.which.co.uk/home-and-garden/kitchen/guides/dishwasher-energy-costs/* [Accessed 7 May 2014]